ACCELERATED BEST PRACTICE

Implementing success in professional firms

Accelerated Best Practice provides an essential toolkit for all professionals managing professional services firms. Faced with ever changing challenges to the successful delivery of the business service offer, this book introduces the idea of a model for success and gives succinct and practical guidance on how to implement strategic and operational change in your organisation. The book is realistic in identifying the challenges faced by an organisation aiming to achieve best practice in service delivery and should be a prerequisite read before starting out on the road to successful implementation.
Senior Civil Engineer, UK Transport Consultancy

Lawyers are trained to deliver expert legal advise but many of us are ill equipped with business skills which hinders our ability to improve efficiency, develop leadership skills, grow our practices and increase profits. Fiona's expertise as a Lawyer and Business coach has inspired our practice to become much more "business street wise ". If you haven't read Fiona's book, you won't know your SWOT from your USP's !!
Managing partner running a local regional law practice

At just over 200 pages this book should almost be regarded as mandatory reading for anyone involved in law firm management, and for anyone who provides advice to law firms, be it management consultancy or financial. It is well written and combines structured analysis with highly perceptive personal views based both on Ms Westwood's time as an equity partner and her subsequent consultancy work with a wide range of professional firms.

For those who read Ms Westwood's previous book, *Achieving Best Practice*, her new book will serve as a very useful refresher in which she moves her ideas and thinking forward. For "Westwood first-timers" they are likely to find it to be something of a revelation – a fascinating and highly perceptive analysis of the problems of management in a professional firm.

Law firm management can be a lonely task and we all need new ideas and inspiration to enable us to undertake the task better. This book is a good source of such ideas and offers clear thinking in a number of areas, in particular the "soft" skill areas that can be so difficult to fully grasp and so easy to neglect.
Andrew Otterburn, Otterburn Legal Consulting
(Journal of the Law Society of Scotland February 2005)

ACCELERATED BEST PRACTICE

Implementing success in professional firms

Fiona Westwood

Matador
9 Priory Business Park
Wistow Road
Kibworth
Leices LE8 0RX
Tel: 0116 279 2299
Email: books@troubador.co.uk
Web: www.troubador.co.uk/matador

ISBN 9781785891076

A Cataloguing-in-Publication (CIP) catalogue record for this book is
available from the British Library

Typeset in 10pt Book Antiqua by Troubador Publishing Ltd, Leicester, UK

Matador is an imprint of Troubador Publishing Ltd

CONTENTS

PREFACE

The Model for Success

Some of you will be familiar with my first book, *Achieving Best Practice – Shaping Professionals for Success* (McGraw-Hill, 2001). It grew out of my frustrations with being part of the management team of a professional service partnership. We used external consultants and undertook formal management training. As a result, we were told we needed to manage our firm better but no one was able tell us how to do it. We looked at management books, seeking advice on putting theory into practice in a professional firm but with limited success. In addition, we found that some of the recommended strategy and human resource tools simply did not work as suggested. For example, when we tried to develop a formal Business Plan, we failed to achieve any kind of consensus from the partners. When we attempted to introduce partner appraisals, this process did not appear to improve morale and performance at all.

Frustrated by this lack of practical help, I resolved to write my own book to provide answers to the challenges of managing a professional firm. Once I moved full time into management consultancy, I supplemented my own experience with detailed research into why some firms were growing and successful in the same market as others who were dying. As a result, I devised the Model for Success for professional service firms.

That was in the year 2000. Fifteen years on, the Model has been applied in a wide range of professional organisations. It has been adapted and improved. This book encapsulates the results of those applications and provides the 'accelerated' Model for use in ambitious firms who want to change and change fast. It provides a holistic view of a professional firm, looks at its internal workings and external focus. Its Segments encompass leadership and management, strategy and processes and provide practical techniques and solutions. They build into a complete circle of knowledge and understanding of management and its application, and deliver the ability to change which is so vitally needed in today's marketplace.

For readers familiar with my first book, Chapters 1 and 2 provide a reminder to the concepts developed there. For new readers, they introduce the Model and its application to professionals and professional practice.

The recession caused many professional firms to focus only on cash-flow. This resulted in short term decisions that may have made the business 'leaner' but not necessarily 'fitter'. Any increase in market activity makes recruiting and retaining skilled people a priority. Mergers and new business structures require considerable management skills. It is important that businesses are resilient by having a clear sense of direction, maintaining a culture where learning is valued, providing sufficient resources to work effectively, focusing on clients and rewarding people who contribute to its success. Specific help with developing resilience can be found in my book, *Developing Resilience – the key to professional success* (Troubador 2010).

ACKNOWLEDGEMENTS

This book reflects what can be achieved by working in partnership with people we trust and respect. I value the help I receive from these relationships. These include all of the professionals and their organisations involved in my research into the Model for Success, as well as my clients who continue to allow me to develop my skills and expertise.

As always, I acknowledge the role my family and friends play in supporting me through the process of creating each of my books.

About the Author

Fiona Westwood graduated LLB (Hons) from Glasgow University in 1974 and became an enrolled solicitor with the Law Society of Scotland in 1976.

During her professional career as a solicitor which spanned 20 years, she had a wide and general experience of client work. This ranged from running a branch office specialising in legal aid through to establishing and running a large commercial property department. In 1987, she was headhunted to help manage an ambitious amalgamation of three long-established law firms, where she had particular responsibility for business development for the new firm.

She set up her own management consultancy in 1994, specialising in working with the professional sector. Her clients include large multi-national practices, niche and regional professional service firms as well as public sector and commercial organisations. Services include strategic coaching, business planning, leadership training and client development projects.

Prior to its publication, McGraw-Hill nominated her book, *Achieving Best Practice – Shaping Professionals for Success*, as their September 2000 Book of the Month. In addition, she writes regularly for business and professional publications and speaks at business conferences in the UK and world-wide.

She has served as a co-opted member of the Practice Management and Client Care Committees of The Law Society of Scotland and as CPE Project Leader on their Education and Training Review and as a Post-Graduate Tutor and Senior Lecturer in Legal Practice at the Glasgow Graduate School of Law and Director of Continuing Professional Education, the School of Law, the University of Glasgow.

To contact her please email faw@westwood-associates.com.

1

INTRODUCTION

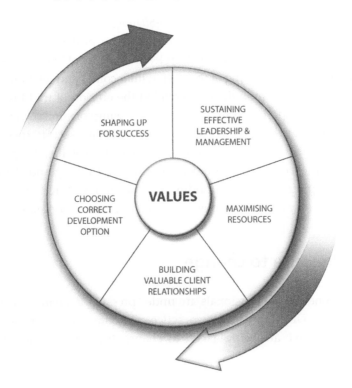

1.1 Introduction

This book is written by a professional for professionals.

It encapsulates my experience of working with professional firms for more than 30 years. I started out in 1974 as a junior professional and learned my trade as a solicitor. Like my peers, I became a more experienced practitioner, developed my technical expertise and client base, and arrived at equity partner with management and business development responsibilities. Juggling family and client commitments, I built a network of contacts and friends. I became more interested in managing my practice than in adjusting commercial leases and decided to switch career tracks. For the past fifteen years, I have worked as a management consultant to all the professions – law, accountancy, surveying, architects, medicine and engineering in particular. Drawing on this experience and expertise has allowed me to develop a Model for Success for professionals and their organisations.

My first book, '*Achieving Best Practice –Shaping Professionals for Success*' was published in 2001. I wrote then that all of the professions seemed to be experiencing drastic reductions in lifestyles and quality of living. Job satisfaction for many had become a thing of the past, with incomes and relationships under severe pressure. Common themes included the erosion of traditional areas of fee income, the impact of technology and increasing consumerism from clients. Whilst recent years have seen feverish activity in many sectors, these pressures continue to affect how we work and how much we enjoy life. Yet, professionals are intelligent people, committed to continuous training and development. What is stopping us from responding in a positive way to these challenges? How can we adapt? What lessons can we learn from other organisations?

1.2   Pressure to change

Like everyone else, professionals are under pressure to change. Regardless of whether we work in private practice, in commercial or not-for-profit organisations, we are being asked to change the way that we deliver our services.

Within my professional life, I have seen long established businesses wither and die, income levels drop alarmingly and workloads increase drastically. In the 1980s, the firm I worked with had an established and loyal client base that paid us without question and left us to get on with the work. Good connections referred us quality work with fees rendered every month without apparent effort or difficulty. Partners enjoyed a pleasant life style active in the local community. They had time for sport, leisure activities and holidays, secure in the knowledge that a stable and dedicated staff could be depended on to keep the business ticking over.

All of this has gone. Client loyalty seems to be a thing of the past with clients shopping around for the best deal, and increasingly litigious if their professional fails to deliver what they want. Clients are better informed and have many sources of information. Professionals are increasingly on the receiving end of bad publicity with stories of 'fat cats', inflated earnings and abuse of their powers. Professional expertise is becoming more complex with constant changes in legislation, regulations and technology. Doing a quality job is now the minimum requirement, with professionals expected to add value to their client relationships and not hide behind a basic professional service.

All professionals are being asked to be more accountable, either to outside bodies and/or for budgets and levels of performance. Their professional bodies, which impose high duties of care, significantly influence professionals. All of this can cause conflict between professional and 'commercial' values. For professionals working in commercial or not-for-profit organisations, financial budgets appear to drive decisions. Professionals are being asked to agree performance levels and work within targets and constraints. Commercial managers often describe professionals as 'devil's advocates', blocking decisions and putting obstacles in their way.

For professional firms, the market remains highly competitive with a resulting downward effect on fees. This puts constant pressure on cash flow and profitability. New business structures challenge the assumptions that used to underlie professional relationships. Relationships between partners may become strained with a lack of trust developing. People seem to have to work harder and harder for less net return. They complain of an absence of job satisfaction and an acceptable standard of living, and of increasing health problems.

1.3   What is the effect?

The effect of this is serious, both in the short and long term. As the world becomes more complex, this requires ever increasing investment in technology, training and communications. As a result, all professionals feel under pressure to develop new skills and adapt their traditional approach to service delivery. They have to cope with increased emphasis on business, budgets and management.

Most professionals are working long hours in an attempt to sustain income levels. They have neither the time nor energy to think creatively, to develop new business connections or new skills. They are reluctant to share client work with others, fearing that they will be forced out of their organisation if they appear not to be needed. This results in people not asking for help, when they are overloaded or in an area outwith their expertise. This can have drastic effects on client services, claims and complaints.

Within firms, tensions are appearing amongst relationships. When trust breaks down, due to declining profits and increasing workloads, a blame culture often develops. This further deprives the firm of any ability to talk issues through or work together to agree the future of the firm. Resources, already under pressure, become increasingly an issue, with senior partners looking to retirement and their pensions, and more junior partners wanting to invest in new technology and ways of working.

Professionals based in the public or private sectors describe similar strains. They can often be in a position of conflict as they try to point out professional issues to managers who appear reluctant to listen to them. Decisions seem to be based on external drivers rather than service quality. They feel that they have to juggle the demands of their organisations with their professional values.

The end result of this is that professionals need help to manage change. Their problems are particular and complex. They need to be able to balance the needs of their clients, their organisations and themselves. Professional partnerships have additional difficulties imposed by their structure, where force of personality can have a powerful influence.

1.4   Who is this book aimed at?

This book is written primarily for professionals, either working in or directly with professional firms. As a result, many are struggling with the 'unmanageability' of partnerships – trying to persuade people to work together, improve profits yet maintain a quality professional service, and attract and retain good clients and staff. Most are faced with increased workloads and accountability.

Professionals often think that their particular problems are unique but, in my experience, these issues are common to the whole professional sector, whether it be accounting, legal, surveying, architecture, engineering, general medical practice or dentistry. The book is therefore applicable to all of the professional sectors, regardless of their trading structure, as lessons can be learned from each other as well as from the external marketplace. It is relevant to those that trade as partnerships, limited companies, and limited liability partnerships, regardless of their size, operational structure or geographical location. It is applicable to all professionals working in professional service organisations, as client demands are common to all.

In addition, this book is relevant to people who work with professionals in any context. This includes commercial organisations as well as not-for-profit situations, including hospitals, universities and colleges. Putting professionals into a traditional management structure can cause 'manageability' problems. Current pressures on these types of organisations include the need to become more commercial. Professionals often see this as a direct challenge to their values and can become at best, mischievous and at worse, disruptive.

1.5   What this book sets out to do

First of all, this book sets out to save us time. I accept that time will be taken up in reading it, but as it contains practical solutions, it allows us to put theory quickly into practice. It saves time by summarising the academic and management theories that are directly relevant to professional service firms. It provides an overview of market trends, allowing us to target our response to them. It provides real life examples of what works in practice, reducing the risk of wasting our time chasing irrelevant issues and ideas.

Each Chapter deals with one aspect of the Model for Success. Chapter 2 summaries the Model in its entirety and introduces key concepts and examples. Chapter 3 provides an overview to allow us to understand and tackle the challenges that we face from current professional and market trends. Chapters 4 to 8 deal with individual segments of the Model, including leadership and management, resources, client relationships, development options and our structure and skills. Chapter 9 provides a summary of the application of the Model in practice and highlights core skills, practical techniques and tools.

At this point, it is worthwhile agreeing some definitions (which will also save us time in later Chapters). When I write about:

'•   professionals', I include all the professions, whether they work in mainstream private practice, commercial and public sector or not for profit organisations,
•   firms' and 'practices', include all organisations which deliver professional services to clients, including those which trade as partnerships, limited companies and limited liability partnerships,
•   clients' includes patients, customers and any other name given to recipients of professional services and whether paid for directly or indirectly, and
•   partner' includes all senior directors and managers.

Secondly, this book sets out to offer reassurance. As we have discussed above, many professionals feel that their working lives are out of control, that clients and external regulations are forcing us to adopt work practices which deprive us of a say in what we are now expected to do. We are repeatedly told that we have to become more businesslike, address risk management, invest in technology and change our traditional ways of working. We seem to constantly need to develop new skills, quite apart from keeping up to date with changes in our technical abilities. As we work our way through this book, we will find out that this is not in fact the case – that a great deal of what we do, know about and have expertise in is in tune with the marketplace and our clients. This offers us the reassurance that we can honour what we as professionals believe in. It also allows us focus our time and energy identifying the necessary changes of emphasis required to dictate how we respond. As a result, we can concentrate on and invest in what we have always considered are the essential elements of professionalism.

Thirdly, this book sets out to develop the ability to manage change. We have already discussed that the professions are experiencing change at an alarming rate. The reasons forcing change can be both positive and negative. They can result from a need to manage growth or respond to new technology, a drive for continuous improvement, and/or a shift in the marketplace. They can also come about as a result of the loss of key people or clients, by changes in funding, and/or by poor profitability or service.

Even where the impetus for change comes as the result of positive reasons, people find it hard to respond. Few people like to move out of their 'comfort zone'. An inappropriate structure and a negative culture can compound these difficulties. People, regardless of their position in an organisation, have a powerful influence on what succeeds and what fails.

Many professional firms are long established serving a wide range of clients. They have inherited a structure, staff and behaviours, adopting a 'family' orientation to the appointment of new partners and the way that they operate. In the past, they were protected from the marketplace and its pressures. Partnership decision-making tends to be cumbersome and firms often have limited management experience. This restricts their ability to respond and makes change difficult to achieve. Professionals and their organisations need to develop this ability. They need to begin to understand the marketplace and take control of it. They need to be able to adjust and respond to it. Key skills include clear leadership, good communications, and a willingness to adapt and learn.

Finally, this book allows us to implement that change. The Model for Success is based on a wheel. The metaphor of the wheel has been chosen with care, because it represents rotation and movement. At the centre of the Wheel are our values around which its five Segments pivot. Working through each of its five Segments creates the ability to change by:

1. building acceptance of and the skills needed for good leadership and management,
2. allowing established work practices to be adapted, people to become more flexible and their skills increase,
3. improving long term client relationships, as well as identifying suggestions for future service delivery,
4. focusing on the development route which fits our individual firm and the marketplace, and
5. adapting our shape and structure, and building our resource and skill base as people become better informed and comfortable with incremental and continuous change.

As a result, it allows our firms to be able to respond positively and quickly, and sustain the momentum of change.

1.6   How manageable are professionals?

From the outset, it is important that we accept that professionals are not easy to manage. Trying to manage them in a typical professional partnership, which often lacks formal structure and sanctions, makes our job even more difficult. Trying to manage partners within those firms who are both owners and fee-earners is nigh impossible. In my experience, even when they intellectually agree that following procedures and working to budgets is appropriate and correct, when it impacts on the way they perform their own work, they simply will not apply it to themselves. Many a managing partner struggles with the 'unmanageability' of his colleagues. Why is this a problem and what can we do about it?

In my view, the answer lies in looking at the essence of professionalism as this underlies every aspect of this book and its successful implementation. Professionals are not easy to manage for a number of reasons inherent in their professional code. We are members of a professional body, which supports us throughout our careers, regardless of where we work, or who we work with. As a member of that body, we must:

- ascribe to a set of core values, which includes client confidentiality,
- share expertise and support each other,
- adhere to a code of conduct which includes ethical behaviour,
- be committed to continuous development and self-improvement,
- put the interests of our clients before our own, and
- honour its rules over and above any personal or organisational demands.

By definition, professionals need to be robust and independent in the advice that they provide and refuse to compromise when they feel that their professional values are being threatened. As a result, they:

- resist being told what to do,
- will be the judge of their competence,
- resent any attempts to impose policies and procedures on them, and
- respond to people that they trust and respect.

This analysis provides some clues to working successfully with professionals and also why some management techniques do not work well. It also provides the key to successful implementation of change. For example, we must start with identifying the core values common to everyone working in the organisation. We must keep referring to them and continue to deliver them. We must not undermine them nor ask people to compromise or disregard them. We must focus on building trust and respect, on encouraging people rather than telling them what to do, and communicating openly and impartially. We also need to educate professionals about management and what it entails.

Many professionals still have little understanding of and as a result, little respect for management. Yet, effective management is an important aspect of success for any business. It involves:

- identifying where the organisation is at present and where it wants to go,
- mplementing a plan of how to get there,
- identifying and sourcing its current and future resources,
- ensuring resources are effectively used and developed,
- responding to any changes needed to sustain the match between current needs and future demands, and
- motivating people within the organisation to support all of the above.

In addition, effective managers must do more than ensure that their organisations run smoothly. They need to provide leadership and a sense of cohesion as well as encourage innovation and change. They must be externally aware, appreciating what is happening in the marketplace and what clients need now and in the future. They also need to be equally skilled in internal operations, having the ability to run the business effectively.

One important element in managing professionals successfully is to identify and resolve any apparent tension between being professional *and* being commercial. In my opinion, for a professional practice to be successful, we must be both. We must be able to provide high quality professional services at a competitive yet profitable rate, so that we can invest in training and technology which, in turn allows us to provide high quality professional services.

However, the test of effective management for any professional firm lies in its ability to implement decisions. This means that professionals have to be motivated to 'buy' into what the organisation is trying to achieve. Otherwise they will stall decision-making and frustrate implementation. Important core skills are therefore those that facilitate decision-making and achieve implementation.

1.7   Implementation is the key to success

This book is designed to save time and it will do so, *if* its suggestions and action points are put into practice. Implementation is therefore the key to success. As a result, it is essential for us to focus on key priorities and action points. It is important therefore to concentrate our efforts on what is important to our particular firm. For example, some of us may have already established strong leadership and management, and may now be struggling with the consistency of client service quality. Others may have recently completed a merger and be coping with managing additional people and resources.

To allow us to position ourselves against the Model and successful organisations, each Chapter ends with a series of Key Action Points. These recommend the key activities required for that segment of the book and require the reader to decide on whether these have been implemented in his or her organisation. If they are already in place, this provides reassurance that this segment has already been implemented. If they are not, they provide a structure for doing so.

In addition, Chapter 9 offers a self-diagnostic exercise as well as a complete Action Plan, detailing how to put the complete Model into effect. This allows readers to position themselves accurately, see in detail how to implement each Segment, step by step and develop an Action Plan to achieve that.

Conclusions

All organisations have to become comfortable with continuous change. Both the marketplace and our clients demand that we change the way we deliver our services and what we can charge for them. However, it is important to develop the ability to do this in a structured way. Failure to address this causes internal tensions over profitability and relationships, and results in people feeling overwhelmed and out of control.

This book is aimed at all professionals. It is designed to allow us to tackle the 'unmanageability' of professionals and professional service firms. To do this, we must harness the strength of our professionalism rather than appear to challenge it.

Key Action Points

1. accept that continuous change is inevitable
2. focus on its positive effects rather than the negative
3. work through each Segment of the Model for Success
4. accept that managing professionals is not easy
5. focus on the strengths of their professionalism
6. select and implement Key Action Points and Plans

2
ACHIEVING BEST PRACTICE

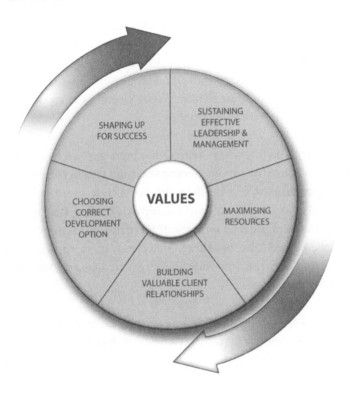

2.1   Introduction

This Chapter introduces readers to the Model for Success. It explains the
background to the Model, introduces us to the core importance of values and
summarises its five individual Segments. It explains the importance of effective
leadership and management, maximising our use of resources, building
valuable client relationships, choosing our development options, and matching
our shape and skills. Each of these Segments is then developed in more depth
in Chapters 4 to 8.

Readers familiar with my first book may wish to use this Chapter to refresh their memories. New readers will be introduced to the thinking behind the Model and its application in practice.

2.2 The Model for Success

The Model is based on my research into a wide range of professionals and professional firms, both in size and service provision across the UK, carried out over a period of more than ten years. Some firms are long established, others more recent. Many have gone through changes of structure, via mergers or amalgamations. Most continue to trade as partnerships, even where there is the option of an alternative trading structure.

This research involved interviews with senior managers and managing partners who were asked about their management style and structure, use of technology, client development and service delivery. Were they more successful if they became limited companies? Was partnership as a trading structure a constraint to growth? Was size of the firm important? Were new firms more successful than long established ones? Was investment in technology rewarded with increased profitability? Had they changed their shape in recent years? Did amalgamations provide a quick way to grow?

As a result, I was able to identify what makes professional firms successful. First and foremost, they are able to change. They may have taken difficult decisions to allow them to do that, but all of them have learned to move forward. In particular, they:

* have leaders and managers who are trusted and respected within the organisation, and well regarded within the business community,
* are aware of their strengths and play to these,
* recognise their weaknesses and tackle these through investment in technology and/or training,
* manage their resources effectively and are able to source additional resources through their networks and/or joint ventures,
* review their client services and adjust their delivery to meet client demands,

- manage their client base well through close and regular contact, and
- most importantly, are able to carry through the changes they decide to implement.

In addition, I found that partnership as a trading structure has a direct influence on the way that firms operate. Used well, it allows the flexibility and speed of response that the modern marketplace demands. Used badly, however, it inhibits decision-making, blocks creativity and damages client services and the way that people operate.

2.3   How do we use it?

Since its inception, the Model for Success has been adjusted and refined. It is based on practical real life experiences of many professional and commercial organisations. As a result, within the confines of client confidentiality, I am able to draw on case studies and examples to illustrate its application in practice. It is structured around the concept of a wheel containing five segments with values at its core. Successful professional organisations need to focus on their values when tackling the implementation of change and must:

1.   sustain effective leadership and management,
2.   maximise their use of resources,
3.   build valuable relationships with their clients,
4.   choose the correct development option, and
5.   adjust their shape and structure to support all of this.

In my experience, each professional organisation is different and has its own style and behaviour. What works with one will not necessarily work with another. I will not and cannot therefore offer prescriptive solutions. I will instead provide practical concepts for firms to apply to their own situation. The strength of professionals and their organisations lies in the variety of styles and approaches that are possible. It is vital therefore that each organisation establishes its own solution. Working through each of the five Segments allows it to position itself against the Model and identify any gaps that are inhibiting its long-term success. Implementing the actions needed to complete each Segment allows its people to see direct benefits and indirectly builds acceptance of change. The Model allows it to become flexible and adaptable but within a structure which keeps it on course, preventing it from wasting time, energy and resources.

2.4   Segment 1 Sustaining effective leadership and management (Chapter 4)

One of the most significant findings from my research is that to be successful, professional organisations must start with effective leadership and management, rather than strategy as most management experts propound. This stems from the nature of professionals, their need for independence and strength of personality. As a result, we can debate strategic options all we like but without the ability to implement these, nothing will ever be achieved. This makes putting in place effective leadership and management our first priority.

Most professional organisations cannot afford the luxury of separating their leadership and management functions. In my opinion, the two are inextricably interwoven with leaders being involved in management and vice versa. The future success of any organisation depends on how well the aspirations of its people match its resources and the marketplace in which it operates. Effective leadership and management work hand in hand, first of all to identify these aspirations and then match (and continue to match) the resources of the business to the needs of the marketplace.

Professionals will only be managed by people who they trust and regard as equals. Professionals refuse to be told what to do. Rather, they have to feel that they are in charge of what they do and how they do it. In addition, they tend to have a jaundiced view of management, seeing it as less important than their technical or client work. They are likely to have had little formal management training and will, as a result, be unaware of what it entails. They often see a conflict between being commercial and being professional. As owners of the business, partners will be reluctant to allow non-partners make decisions. Senior professionals often feel that commercially-focused managers interfere with their ability to service clients. All of this causes resentment and frustration, with such managers complaining to me that their advice is not heeded and their abilities and experience ignored. Many quit after two or three years of 'being sidelined or marginalised'. It is therefore vital that management is recognised as having an important role in the firm.

The test of effective management for a professional firm lies in its ability to implement any decision taken. This means that professionals have to 'buy in' to what the organisation is trying to achieve. Otherwise they will stall decision-making and frustrate implementation. Key management skills are therefore those that facilitate decision-making. These include the ability to:

1.   inspire trust and build relationships,
2.   influence people without the use of direct authority,
3.   deal with the impact of behaviour,
4.   tackle conflict constructively,
5.   communicate effectively and listen actively, and
6.   solve problems and achieve long term solutions.

All of these will be developed in more detail in Chapter 4.

2.4 1 The crucial importance of values

As we can see from the diagram of our Model for Success, values lie at the core of everything that we do. As a result, we must first of all identify and then apply a set of values common to our organisation and the people working within it. Effective leadership and management therefore require the identification of these values. This may seem self-explanatory and common sense, but, in my experience, discussions about values rarely happen as most organisations would see this as 'too soft an issue' and fraught with difficulties.

How do we define values? In my view, values are those enduring principles that we hold dear and directly influence our behaviour. One of the best ways to identify our own values is to consider why we left a previous organisation. What was it that finally made us say enough is enough? Was it that we were unhappy about the way people were being treated (values of consideration, respect for others and teamwork)? Or that financial considerations appeared to be paramount (values of job satisfaction or duty to society)? Or that the firm seemed to be completely unaware of the importance of treating people fairly (values of security, trust and respect for others)?

Value conflicts can have a significant effect on us as individuals. They can be strong enough to make us leave an organisation. They can affect our health and well-being as well as have a damaging effect on our organisations.

Table 2.4.1(a) considers what happens when values are not delivered, and the effect this has on us and our organisations. This analysis is grouped into four value sections – our professional body's, our organisational, our professional and our private values. If the values of our professional body are not delivered, the organisation will suffer from complaints, rigorous inspections and a poor reputation. As a result, it will have difficulty in recruiting quality staff. If the values of the organisation are not delivered, it will experience friction, poor communications and fragmented client support. If the professional values of individuals are not delivered, then there will be little sharing of expertise, a lack of trust generally with the good people (who can get positions elsewhere) likely to leave. With private values not delivered, people may have health and stress-related problems.

Table 2.4.1(b) considers what happens when values are delivered. If those of our professional body are delivered, the firm will meet its compliance requirements, enjoy a good reputation and image and as a result, be able to attract quality people to work with it. It will also receive advice and support from that body, which may include advance notice of compliance changes, key trends and market influences. If the organisation's values are delivered, it will have consensus, people will work well together, client service will be co-ordinated and effectively delivered, the organisation will be well resourced and have growth potential.

If the professional values of individuals are delivered, the organisation will enjoy commitment and energy from these people, who will share clients and expertise. If private values are delivered, the firm will have healthy, balanced individuals who will be outward looking, innovative and responsive to change. It is important that all four boxes are equally balanced with all receiving equal emphasis.

This analysis shows the importance of ensuring the delivery of values. Let us look at its application in one area of common conflict of values – between being both commercial *and* professional.

Many professionals think that business people are unethical and put their own needs above those of their customers. Professionals on the other hand feel that they work selflessly for ungrateful clients. Couple all of this with a lack of understanding about what management entails and the normal defensive reaction to change, and we begin to see why professionals block so many commercial decisions. It is essential to bring this apparent 'conflict' out into the

Table 2.4.1(a) Values Matrix - where values are not delivered

	Internal Impact	External Impact
Organisational Values	ORGANISATIONAL if not delivered, will have friction, tensions, factions, lack of resources, poor communications with staff, fragmented client support	PROFESSIONAL BODY if not delivered, will have complaints, rigorous inspections, time taken up with responding, problems over recruitment of quality staff
Individual Values	PROFESSIONAL if not delivered, will have stress, lack of trust, openness or sharing of expertise, limited innovation, bad behaviour and /or likely to leave	PRIVATE if not delivered, will have health and stress problems

Table 2.4.1(b) Values Matrix – where values are delivered

	Internal Impact	External Impact
Organisational Values	ORGANISATIONAL if delivered, will have consensus, vision, resources, client satisfaction, growth	PROFESSIONAL BODY if delivered, will have compliance, support, reputation, quality recruitment
Individual Values	PROFESSIONAL if delivered, will have commitment, quality, job satisfaction, enjoyment, happy to share knowledge and develop others	PRIVATE if delivered, will have health, balance, contentment

open, as in my experience, most of the issues can be resolved or may be based on a misunderstanding.

It is important therefore to structure a 'Commercial versus Professional debate', which is often the first opportunity that people have had to talk about this. What starts out as a long list of alleged issues often dissolves into an enhanced understanding of the drivers behind the organisation as well as agreement on apparent areas of difficulty. To undertake this exercise, firms should draw up two Value boxes – those of commercial organisations and those of professional organisations and then compare the two. There may in fact be many similarities. For example, both will value high quality client delivery, both will value the skills and expertise of their people and the resources to support that. Highlighting these similarities reinforces that people have a great deal in common. Addressing any outstanding conflicts helps to reassure people that leadership and management are effective.

2.4 2   How to identify our values?

Identification of core values need not be as difficult as professionals sometimes make out. In my view, it should not require several days away from the office, or endless hours of discussion. Indeed, it can be completed in a couple of hours, with some thought, pre-work and preparation. It involves two stages, first of all the collating of a composite list of possible values and secondly, voting on their selection.

First of all, we need to source some possible suggestions. Most professional organisations have websites and promotional literature. These will contain some 'value' words, and provide us with a starting point. (Interestingly, one firm I worked with took exception to this approach as external marketing people had written this copy for them. It is important to remember that what we hold out to clients as our values is what we actually believe in.) Other sources of information are SWOT analyses (see later in this Chapter) that often contain value words, as well as noticing the value words people use when asked to talk about their organisations. These sources allow a tentative list to be prepared which the partners and main stakeholders must debate and vote on.

First of all, people should be asked to add their own suggestions to generate a composite list of at least 20 words. From this list, people are asked to choose their individual 'Top Ten'. These individual lists are then collated to produce a core list of three to seven values which a high percentage of people agree on. These again should be discussed as there may be a number that are not so highly rated but a majority of people feel are important enough to be included. The aim is to produce a final list that people agree form the core values of the organisation. I usually find there is a tendency for people to assume that all professional organisations will have the same values i.e. quality, integrity, financial robustness, but in my experience, this is not the case. For example, some professional organisations will rank team-working much higher than others who will prefer valuing individual expertise.

What can we call this framework of values? The phrase 'mission statement' has developed a fairly bad press, with people feeling that the words often bear little relevance to the reality of working in that organisation. However, the creation of such a frame of reference is important as it forces an organisation to reflect on what is core to its beliefs and values. Rather than talk about mission statements, I prefer discussions around 'Commonality of Purpose'. This encourages people to talk about why they work together, what is important to them now and in the future. This 'Commonality of Purpose' by its very creation, will be personal to individual organisations. Some examples I have seen include:

- we are committed to supplying high quality support to clients,
- we work with clients who value what we do for them,
- we care about our clients and our people,
- we adopt an innovative approach to client services,
- we believe in teamwork and reward people accordingly.

Most organisations find completing this exercise very reassuring as agreeing core values reinforces that people do want to contribute to the organisation and its long-term success.

2.4 3 Developing trust

The second key to successful leadership and management is the ability to develop trust. This links in strongly with values, as one of the reasons we trust people is because they share our values. As indicated before, professionals will only work with people that they trust. In addition, they resent any attempt to directly control their work. This emphasises the need for leaders and managers to inspire trust rather than impose control and takes us back to the comments above about the need to deliver values so as to generate that trust.

The leadership skills of inspiring trust are difficult to define. We all know that there are some people we inherently trust and others who from the outset we are uncomfortable with. How do we know who we can trust? How do we access background information to help us with that assessment?

First of all, we can formally debate and agree a set of core values as we have discussed above. Secondly, we can look at people's past performance and track-record. Most professionals operate in strong 'closed shop' networks. This means that we find out about the history of people – often knowing who they worked with in the past, which organisations they trained in and the type of client services they have been involved with. As a result, we are able to quickly tap into first hand knowledge of that individual and his or her 'professionalism' and are therefore much more likely to trust people we can track in that way. Thirdly, professionals tend to use jargon, often as a short-hand way of communicating but also as a way of assessing people's knowledge of them and how they operate. Again, they are more willing to trust people who 'speak their language'. This also helps to illustrate the difficulty that commercial managers or professionals from other disciplines have when trying to manage professional firms. Without working with them for many years, it is not easy for external managers to convince professionals of their worth.

Finally, as with any relationship, one of the best ways of developing trust is by being willing to listen to people and as a result, leaders and managers must place a lot of emphasis on this. However, listening is not enough. Having listened, effective management requires a response – based on reasoned analysis and consistent judgement. Good leaders and managers must seek to be respected, not liked. Open communications are therefore an important element in the establishment of trust. Another essential element is being consistent, which is greatly helped by formal planning.

2.4.4 Planning

Most professional firms now have some kind of written business plan or summary of key objectives. The ability to plan in a formal way is an essential management tool as, in my experience, ineffective management results from being partial in the way decisions are taken and implemented. Especially within partnerships, planning can therefore give a sense of cohesion, consistency and a common purpose with written plans providing a frame of reference against which to make short and long-term decisions. It allows us to take control of the marketplace rather than allowing the market to control us. It also encourages the consideration of what resources are needed and how these should be allocated and co-ordinated. This in turn increases productivity and awareness of the costs and benefits of these resources and as a result, builds co-operation and understanding.

Planning implies a structured and logical approach to where the firm is and where it wants to go. Not all planning needs to be formal, but I would recommend that for professional firms, where there are a number of owners, it is important to formalise what is agreed in writing and quickly. There is no absolute template for a written Business Plan (see suggested template in the Appendix to this Chapter) but the general headings should include:

1. an introduction to the firm, the purpose of the plan and its intended audience,
2. an analysis of the current business,
3. a review of its past performance,
4. a review of current and future market trends,
5. a picture of where it wants to go, including long term strategic objectives,
6. a practical action plan of how it is going to get there and
7. its financial projections.

This appears at first glance to involve a lot of work. However, the Plan can be built up over time and once the initial one has been completed, it is a much quicker task to keep it up-to-date, adjust and agree future plans. The Segments of the Model for Success are therefore designed to facilitate the development of the Plan by allowing us to carry out detailed analysis of key sections such as resources, clients and the marketplace.

2.5 Segment 2 Maximising our resources (Chapter 5)

Many organisations fail to develop as a result of having a limited appreciation of resource management and what that entails. This includes a lack of understanding of pricing, overheads, working capital, cash flow, and quality of their services. Some fail because they overtrade, taking on too much work and/or work which is unprofitable for them, and as a result, confuse being busy with being successful. Others fail because their owners are inflexible and autocratic, refusing to seek outside advice.

To be able to change, any organisation needs an established resource base. This has to include not only the traditional hard resources of balance sheet assets, such as capital and equipment but also the softer resources of good communications and working relationships. To use its resources well, the organisation needs to be aware of its strengths and weaknesses, its external market opportunities and pressures. This requires careful analysis of all aspects – its systems and people, working capital, client base and future potential.

Most people reading this book will be familiar with a SWOT Analysis (this common sense checklist has been used for many years, for example, see Tilles, 1968). This considers the internal Strengths and Weaknesses of the organisation and its external Opportunities and Threats. An example of a typical professional firm is shown in Table 2.5.

Although apparently simple, completion of such an analysis is a worthwhile exercise as it provides a useful overview of the firm. It is worthwhile expanding the list of people involved in this exercise beyond the partners and senior managers. It is useful to obtain the views of the younger professionals, support staff and even clients and contacts as to what they think. Their involvement also helps to open up communications especially within the firm, educating people and building commitment to use resources well. Debate on its findings is also important as it means that sensitive issues have to an objective structure to be explored.

2.5.1 Informed discussions

The best way to do this is to work from factual information, rather than people's perceptions. In my experience, strong-minded professionals tend to turn their subjective opinions into 'hard facts'. For example, statements like *'he never does any work!'* or *'that department is a complete waste of space!'* can commonly be heard at management and partner meetings.

As a result, it is important to gather as much objective information as possible

Table 2.5 SWOT analysis

STRENGTHS	WEAKNESSES
well established wide range of services premises well-sited & good appearance loyal & stable staff good quality client base good range of partners – age & expertise good local reputation operates efficiently adequate IT systems good relations with funders good internal working relations well-rounded management team access to external referrals and contacts	traditional fee areas declining not specialised structure not working well patchy computer skills lack of agreed direction communications poor decisions take too long lack of client awareness of all services lack of consistency of approach current work levels too high dependence on outside IT support
OPPORTUNITIES	THREATS
local connections wide range of services specialist services joint ventures with other professionals	increased pressure on traditional fee areas fees overall being driven down increased competition from other firms increasing complexity of work increased competition from non-professional sources

to be able to discuss these issues from a *basis of fact*. Yes, some of us will instinctively know what needs to be done, but obtaining hard data allows these areas to be discussed objectively rather than subjectively. This provides the benefit of de-personalising the debate, which is extremely important in dealing with partnerships where any erosion of trust can be damaging in both the short and long term. The ultimate aim of any analysis is to make decisions about the way the business operated and the services it provides.

2.5.2 The Resource Audit

The hard data recommended above comes from a Resource Audit of the organisation. This looks:

1. people
2. finance
3. pricing and service levels
4. suppliers
5. administration and systems
6. client base
7. quality
8. competitors and
9. external resources.

The Table 2.5.2 illustrates some of the questions that need to be asked. It is worthwhile at this point taking 30 minutes to work out the answers as they apply to your firm.

The *process* of completing the analysis is as important as the information itself. By obtaining and working through the collation of information, people become more knowledgeable about the organisation as a whole, the details of its operations and the interconnection of different elements. In addition, different groupings of people become more comfortable with working together and sharing views. It need not be a daunting and time-consuming exercise as basic information should already exist in separate reporting systems such as management accounts, performance and client management reports. The analysis can make use of this and make it more relevant and applied through linking them all together.

Completing such an Audit allows the firm to prepare an Action Plan to tackle areas where resources are not being used well. For example, it knows which areas of work are profitable, and which are not. This allows it to consider whether it can make areas more profitable by, for example, delegating work to para-professionals or by using IT more intensively. It knows which clients add value and which do not, what clients expect from the firm and where its services can be adjusted to match these expectations. People can now take decisions to change on an informed basis. The information itself should not dictate the decision, but help to facilitate an impersonal discussion of the options. These

Table 2.5.2 Resource Audit

1 people	how effectively are individuals working? how effectively are departments working? how effective is cross department support? do we have excess capacity? do we have areas under pressure? where is training required?
2 finance	how quickly are we producing up-to-date information? how accessible is it? how accurate is our working capital information? how effective is our debt recovery? what is causing late/non-payment of fees? what are our current levels of work-in-progress? how recoverable are they? are we asking for payments to account and early payment of outlays? how consistent are our recovery procedures? how will we fund future capital purchases?
3 pricing and service levels	what is our feeing policy? are we feeing at profitable levels? on what basis are we setting fees, e.g. cost? what clients will pay? as a response to the levels set by competitors? what are the profitable areas of our business? what are our current service levels? should we be outsourcing areas of work?
4 suppliers	are we purchasing effectively? how can we eliminate excess usage/wastage? are our leasing arrangements cost effective? can we do more for ourselves in-house?
5 administration and systems	who is responsible for making decisions about administration? do we use our office space effectively? do we have the right equipment in the right places? do we have the correct software packages? are people using them fully? are we too dependent on external IT support?

Table 2.5.2 Resource Audit (cont.)

6 client base	why do our clients come to us? why do our clients stay with us? why have clients left us? where do we have expertise? what are we known for? which clients are profitable? do we have the right mix of services?
7 quality	what are issues arising out of claims/complaints? how do our clients define the quality of our service? what elements add value to them? what elements do they take for granted? what external benchmarks can we develop?
8 competitors	who are our direct competitors? who are our indirect competitors? how well do we compare on price, location, range and quality of services? how can we effectively compete with them? how can we make adjustments to improve our competitive position?
9 external resources	who provides us with external resources? what do they provide e.g. finance, information, referrals? how reliable are they? do we reciprocate and support them in return? what additional resources do we need? how will we source them?

options must reflect the values of the firm, and may therefore require, for example, that some services be retained regardless of their profitability.

It is essential not only to identify, but also to implement some key actions as this starts the firm on the road to success and builds momentum and acceptance of change. It also proves to people that change is possible. This segment of the

Model is crucial to starting the process of change as it provides the key to 'unsticking' accepted work practices and behaviours, and undermining ill-founded assumptions and attitudes. It allows the wheel to start turning. It also prevents the firm from going off down the wrong road because a few strong-minded and opinionated individuals advocate it.

2.6 Segment 3 Building valuable client relationships (Chapter 6)

This Segment of the Model looks at the importance of building valuable relationships with our clients. Historically, professionals were criticised for a lack of client awareness, of not being accessible and running their organisations to suit themselves rather than their clients. It used to be possible for professionals to set their own timetables for workloads, with clients prepared to wait for a 'considered response'. More recently, however, increased competition has encouraged them to become more client-focused.

Professionals now complain of a lack of client loyalty, with clients shopping around for the 'best deal'. Clients have become more demanding, no longer prepared to wait for consultations and appointments. Client work itself has become more complex and technical, with numerous changes in rules and regulations every year. The introduction of email, in particular, has meant that response times have been significantly reduced. As a result, many professionals currently work long hours with limited control over their working days and weeks. Symptoms of stress and overwork are now common. How do we reconcile this with finding the quality of time and energy to give tailored and difficult advice?

2.6.1 Asking our clients

We care about our clients and the services we render. As a result, most professionals are committed to providing a high quality professional service. This is the minimum clients expect from us and rightly so. They are paying us for our professional judgement and expertise – to listen to their needs and respond to them.

However, one fundamental change of focus is required before we proceed with the rest of this discussion. It is *the client* who is the judge of the level of our service, not us. This is often very difficult for firms to appreciate. They will talk a great deal about the importance of being client-focused, but by that they mean delivering the level of service and/or type of services that *they think* the client wants. However, to build relationships valuable to both parties requires that we investigate and then deliver *what the client* defines as a high quality professional service. Once this mind-shift has been achieved, it is much easier to focus on delivering what clients value.

We cannot assume that we know what clients want from us. We need to ask them what services they want and how they want them to be delivered. This may require us to restructure our firms to match. For example, whilst a department structure might suit our areas of expertise and feeing policies, clients may not like dealing with a number of people within the firm and receiving fee notes charged on a different basis. Clients may prefer one point of contact and one rate of charge.

As a result, we have to start by asking our clients what they value. This takes us into the vexed area of client satisfaction questionnaires and surveys. Most professionals are reluctant to 'open the box' of asking clients what they think of their service. Some send out satisfaction questionnaires at the end of a file, asking for comments about basic services, such as how quickly the phones and e-mails were answered. In my experience, these often provide limited responses and even more limited useful data. What is more important, in my view, is to ask clients more open questions about what they think of the services provided, for example, in terms of timeliness and/or value for money. We need to tackle this in a structured way by completing a Client Service Audit. Table 2.6.1 illustrates the types of questions that can be asked of both new and existing clients.

Rather than using questionnaires where the answers are often difficult to interpret and may result in incomplete information, firms should speak directly to certain key clients and/or groups of clients. This can be done informally at the end of a routine meeting or over lunch, or can be carried out more formally, through end-of-project reviews. Many firms now accept the importance of continuing client contact by appointing 'Key Client Partners,' where one partner is put in charge of co-ordinating all the work being done for a particular client or group of clients. This allows ongoing discussions about level of service delivery distinct from discussions about a particular piece of work. It also helps

Table 2.6.1 The Client Service Audit

New clients	What made you select our firm?
	If you changed professionals in the last two years, why did you change?
	What do you look for in a good professional?
Current clients and services	Did the project achieve what you expected? If not, why not?
	Did you feel that you received value for money? If not, why not?
	What went well?
	What could we have done better?
	How could our level of face-to-face contact be improved upon?
	How could our communications with you be improved?
	What would you describe as the firm's strengths?
	What would you describe as the firm's weaknesses?
	What other services could we have provided you with?
Future Services	In what areas do you anticipate your level of work with us will increase or decrease over the next 2-5 years?
	In what other areas will you be seeking professional support in the next 2-5 years?
	How would you like these provided and by whom?
	How would you define a 'quality' professional service?
	What could professionals in general do better?

to maintain a client overview where a number of fee earners are working on different files. It can also be achieved through targeted focus groups or involving clients in more general discussions about the future direction of the firm. Some firms prefer to use external consultants to carry this through on their behalf, on the basis that clients may find it easier to speak to a third party. Whilst some clients may prefer not to speak directly with the firm, in my view, the disadvantage with this approach is that there is no opportunity for both sides to develop and build on their existing *personal* relationship.

Once they have overcome their initial reluctance, firms are often surprised about the amount of useful and positive information such sessions provide, not only about current services, but also what the client will want from the firm in the future. Some have found out about fundamental concerns about personnel, response rates or costs. Others have identified the potential for new services.

What is essential is that having gathered the information, we need to act on it by taking corrective action. If clients have taken the time to give us the information, they need to see tangible proof of listening and responding to what they have suggested. Client loyalty needs to be developed and nurtured – not taken for granted.

2.6.2 Delighting the customer!

Many management gurus emphasise the importance of not just satisfying but *'delighting the customer'*. None of us would disagree with this if we think how annoying it is to buy a new car and still have to pay for a full tank of petrol when we pick it up!

Yet, we often have to give clients information that they would rather not hear and/or are blamed by the client for a problem which is not our fault. Sometimes, we are dealing with clients who do not want to consult us in the first place. They have not chosen to select our services but have been forced by circumstances or by the behaviour of others to seek our advice. Others see us as a necessary evil – something they have to do. Even where they do actively choose to use us, sometimes we cannot deliver the solution they want or achieve a successful resolution of their situation. In addition, we may well have to charge them for our work, even if it provides no return to them at all. In all of these circumstances it is impossible to *'delight them'*. At best, we may be able to provide with a result which they can tolerate. At worst, despite doing our utmost for them, we will still be blamed for not delivering what they had hoped to achieve.

We need therefore to be very careful of attempting to *'delight our customers'*. As a result, we need to focus on providing a service which:

- delivers the best solution to the client at a fee which is acceptable to them, and *at the same time*
- allows us to deliver a professional service at a price which is profitable to us.

That may require some readjustment of the clients' expectations as well as a discussion about costs. As will be developed in more detail in Chapter 6, both of these should be tackled as early in the relationship as possible.

Step 1   Establish and agree clients' expectations

Some professionals shy away at the outset of a consultation to explain the pros and cons of the particular client situation, preferring to make vague assurances about likely outcomes. However, if we are to develop and maintain a long-term client relationship, we must establish from the outset what we can and cannot achieve for them, how long it may take and how much it is likely to cost.

The explaining of options, procedures and costs must be done sympathetically. Too often professionals, inured to the content of their work, forget how clients feel when they seek professional advice. To help us remember this, we need to think how we feel when we consult another professional for personal reasons. Clients are usually anxious about their situation and may have had to screw up their courage to contact us. Personal clients may not have used our services for some years. Even clients who use on a regular basis feel under pressure for one reason or another. As a result, we must take the time to 'settle' the client, to appreciate that they may be unhappy and worried and not assume that any antipathy or 'prickliness' is directed at us.

Step 2   Develop and retain trust

The essence of developing and successfully managing relationships is based from the outset on our ability to develop and retain trust. However, increasing pressure on profits has caused many professionals to worry about putting clients off at the outset by explaining in detail what will be involved. The result is that clients leave early meetings with a sense of euphoria that the magic wand does exist and that everything will soon be rosy. Frustration then seeps in, as they are asked for more and more detailed information, with time passing without apparently being any nearer a resolution. The client becomes disaffected, looking for sinister reasons in the delay –seeing it as evidence of a lack of competence on the part of the professional, a way of milking fees and being '*taken for a ride*' or '*of having the wool pulled over one's eyes*'.

Indeed, even when the professional is following the normal path at the best speed possible, client relations will become strained because the client was not alerted to this at the outset. On top of this, professionals are not good at being proactive in communicating with clients, preferring to wait until they have something positive to say. This can create a tension, which is not healthy – and if things start to go wrong for any reason, can lead to strained relationships.

Step 3 Responsive to their needs

The next vital element is to make clients feel that we are 'responsive' to their needs. To do this, we have to listen to them – to understand what is important to each particular client and what motivates him or her. This takes time initially – but it is time well spent as it will help to develop a long-term relationship, and result in reducing the need for and the amount of communication. It is also the opportunity to introduce the client at the beginning of the project to the concept that we are not accessible 24 hours every day. It is important to explain that there will be occasions when we cannot be interrupted (as for example, when in a meeting with another client). As a result, there will be times when the client will not be able to deal with us directly. It is important at the outset to introduce them the person whom we *trust* to deal with the client, as the client must not feel that he or she is being fobbed off with second best.

Additionally, this is an important stage from the marketing point of view. We know that the client has come to see us about the problem in hand. We should check why he or she has selected our firm and us in particular. This is essential information for the firm, and helps to build up an action plan to attract future work. It is equally important at this point to give the client information about the firm and all the services that it offers. We must not assume that clients know what we do, as in my experience, clients continue to express confusion about what individual professionals actually do. For example, a property professional may be able to distinguish between one type of surveying service and another, but not everyone can. As a result, we need to give clients background about the firm, its style and approach and what additional services we can provide. This brings us onto the next Segment – consideration of what strategy we want to adopt.

2.7   Segment 4 Choosing the correct development option (Chapter 7)

Most writers on business strategy make much use of the phrase 'strategic management'. By that, they mean that organisations need to decide their future direction and find the resources to get them there. Segments 1, 2 and 3 of the Model have provided us with a detailed understanding of our values, resources and clients. We now need to move on to analyse the marketplace and develop our understanding of it to allow us to choose the correct options for developing the firm. To do this, we need to be able to identify what future clients of the firm will want from us. This requires knowledge of market trends.

Given the resource base of most professional firms, it is unlikely that we can directly influence the marketplace. It is essential therefore that we develop ways of coping with its variations. Increasing consumerism and the impact of IT, in particular, have resulted in professionals feeling overwhelmed by pressure to adapt and change. Many people are confused about *how* to respond, unable to prioritise which of these pressures are capable of being managed and controlled. People seem generally aware that *'things are not what they were'*. Some firms feel unable to plan ahead, arguing *'there is little point as things change so fast'*. Some people are uneasy and want clarity. Others appear to be blindly indifferent. Most firms want to be more in control and to have some sense of what needs to be done. How can we have any long-term plan for the business when things change so fast?

Strategic planning is important as it can help to:

- put issues into perspective,
- allow us to make an assessment of their impact and importance,
- identify some positive (defensive or proactive) steps to be taken,
- allow discussions based on an informed position rather than subjective bias, and
- focus decision-making.

In addition, it allows us to think in a strategic way about our firm and its future potential.

2.7.1 Strategic thinking

Thinking strategically requires two elements – structured analysis and lateral thinking. This reflects the two sides of our brain – the 'left' or analytical side and the 'right' or creative side. Everyone in the firm should be encouraged to be more externally aware as there is always a risk that we become so focused on the narrow areas in which we work that we miss something which could have a significant impact on us and the way that we work. Reading widely, talking to other professions and sectors and keeping an eye open generally are all excellent sources of information about future trends and developments.

However, it is important to focus our attention on the development of strategic choices. In summary, developing strategies for the future of the firm includes the following steps:

1. analysing the marketplace to identify significant trends,
2. developing some choices by thinking innovatively,
3. checking these choices against our values,
4. checking them against our resources (current and future),
5. choosing an option,
6. selecting the best way of achieving it,
7. implementing it, and
8. reviewing progress and adjusting if required.

Depending on the size of the firm, I would suggest that a Strategy Group be established or an individual be given responsibility to generate ideas and report regularly to the whole firm. Firstly, people who enjoy analysis and structure should be made responsible for watching for trends in the marketplace, including changes in clients' demands and competitors. Secondly, those within the firm who enjoy lateral and conceptual thinking should be encouraged and allowed to do so in the particular context. This is a different exercise than the trend analysis, as it requires 'out-of-the box' thinking. These two groups should report on their findings and suggestions to the firm as a whole to provide the opportunity to consider these trends, debate these ideas, agree or disagree and select some options. This 'Options Debate exercise' is important as it helps to educate people about the reasons why change may be needed, the choices available and based on factual data and analysis, provides the framework for rational debate. It also allows the firm to identify options in good time to be able to respond to them as well as find the resources, the skills and expertise to carry them through.

Market analysis and choices will be developed in more detail in Chapter 7, but it is worthwhile at this stage to look in general terms at what is available.

2.7.2 What choices do we have?

There is a range of strategic choices open to most organisations. At the simplest level, these include:

- selling more of our existing services to our existing clients,
- selling our existing services to new clients,
- selling new services to existing clients,
- moving into a completely new market for both services and clients, or
- giving up all together!

Within the current marketplace, most professional firms are under continuous pressure to improve profit levels. To do this, some may be happy to maintain current fee levels but reduce operational costs. Others may already be tightly managed but want to accelerate their profit growth. First of all, therefore, we need to decide which is our priority. For example, are we happy with the firm the size it is, but want to increase our profitability? Or do we want to grow bigger, increase turnover and hopefully our profits?

Some professional firms have successfully adopted a competitive strategy based on offering the lowest costs. This has validity as long as it is consciously adopted and not merely the result of external pressures to reduce the level of fees charged. Given the personal nature of professional services, a strategy based on differentiation from our competitors makes commercial sense. A niche strategy can work well as it allows the firm to position itself in the market, focusing its attention on a specific sector. This suits the limited resource base of smaller organisations, as well as allowing the firm to more easily target its profile and image-raising activities.

Which choice to select *must* reflect its values and resources. Carrying out a 'Practicality Check' at this point is essential. Does our proposed choice reflect our values as these provide a constant frame of reference? Do we have or can we access sufficient resources to implement our choice? To a certain extent, current resources will influence what is possible, but the organisation may select an option that involves expanding the resources considerably. That will then become an important element in the route that the firm takes to get there.

2.7.3 How are we going to get there?

There are a number of ways of implementing any major strategy or change of emphasis for the firm. Common methods include organic growth, which provides the advantage of stability and the disadvantage of slowness, or one of the more adventurous and faster options of amalgamations or joint ventures.

Choice 1   Organic Growth

Organic growth implies the steady and incremental development of the firm, building on its inherent strengths and addressing its weaknesses. In my experience, some firms have been very successful with this approach and have more than maintained their market position. However, this option is becoming increasingly difficult for two main reasons. Firstly, this response may be too slow for many of the current market pressures. For example, firms are being forced to invest heavily in technology, putting pressure on capital and ways of working. Smaller firms may find it difficult to fund such investment. Increasing complexity is putting pressure on professionals to become more specialised, which encourages firms to become more selective in the clients they serve.

The other reason is that younger professionals are simply more mobile and less likely to be enticed by the carrot of partnership than their previous generation. They may think that the time to achieve partnership is too long and uncertain and therefore question the risk and reward equation. In addition, it is much more professionally acceptable to move between firms. All of this means that it can be difficult for firms to grow organically by retaining quality people as good professionals can always find positions elsewhere. If too many people come and go, the firm takes on the appearance of itself being unstable. Existing partners may become unwilling to delegate their client work to younger members of the team, fearing that they will leave and take the clients with them. This produces severe problems of manageability. Senior people hold on to work they should delegate with the result that young professionals will not be allowed the chance to improve their skills, and may become unsettled and leave.

The organisation's ability to retain high quality people is the key to growing organically. This requires involving young professionals in long-term discussions, talking to them regularly on a one-to-one basis, recognising their contribution and giving them the opportunity to learn. They will then respond positively to being given responsibility, and challenging and quality client work, supported by more senior professionals.

Choice 2   Accelerated Growth

A second strategic choice is to decide to accelerate the growth of the firm. Methods to achieve this include buying or merging with another firm or entering into some kind of formal relationships with other organisations. All of this is developed in more detail in Chapter 7. In summary, each method has distinct advantages and disadvantages, but whatever route is chosen must bring positive benefits to the firm, which may include:

- increasing the overall profile of the firm,
- increasing the partner profile,
- increasing the skill base and expertise,
- providing succession planning and/or an exit strategy,
- increasing the resource base,
- producing economies of scale,
- increasing the quality and depth of the client base,
- increasing the future potential of the client base, and/or
- providing geographical or service expansion.

It is too easy at the outset to assume that some of these must happen by default. As a result, it is important to identify which benefits will be delivered by the merger option and develop ways of measuring whether they have been achieved.

2.7.4 Putting it into practice

Once the choice has been made, it has to be implemented. This is the area where most firms get into difficulty. Organisations may be good at analysing the marketplace, spend a great deal of money (often on consultancy fees) and energy generating options, and then fail to carry any of them through. They may start a change programme or initiative with a great deal of hype and then face fundamental problems in getting people to respond.

In my experience, whatever is proposed *must* reflect the core values of the organisation. If this is not done, people will block any attempt to implement the new programme or approach. As a result, it is important to show how this option fits within the overall values of the organisation and allows these values to be supported and maintained. Another common failure stems from a lack of understanding of the amount of resources (time, energy) or change of skills and attitude required. Both of these should have been identified in the 'Practicality Check' we discussed earlier. It takes time to carry through any strategic choice. As a result, it is important not to lose focus and enthusiasm. It is better to split its implementation down into a number of steps all working towards a common goal, and as a result, be able to review and *demonstrate* progress regularly. Any interim successes and achievements should be promulgated to everyone in the organisation to keep the momentum going and show that things do happen.

We now need to look at matching our shape and structure to support the choices we have made.

2.8   Segment 5 Shaping up for success (Chapter 8)

This segment of the Model for Success concentrates on shaping our organisations to meet our current demands and future expectations. Structure plays an important role in facilitating the success of professional firms. Their structure tends to be different from other types of organisations who often operate hierarchically, with people having different levels of authority depending on their position. Professional firms traditionally lack such structure and often 'confuse' ownership, management and technical operations.

This 'confusion' leads to problems for both operational and strategic management. The shape of an organisation can directly influence the way it currently operates as well as its future direction or strategy. The structure of an organisation is a reflection of its values and resource base and will also determine its potential flexibility. Structure will therefore have a direct effect on what strategy or change of direction can be achieved. As a result, it is important that strategy and structure support each other. For example, there is little point in adopting a cross-department team approach to client services if the firm is structured along rigid department lines with poor communications and a separate basis of charging. As a result, clients are unlikely to experience a seamless service.

The 'shape' of the firm includes the people within the firm. We need therefore to consider how to shape and develop new partners, how to deal with succession issues and how to encourage people to 'grow'. Our structure is important when we consider the implementation of strategy. For example, our structure will be different if we had decided to target 'high volume, low skill' client work from that which services 'low volume, high skill' levels. Structure plays an integral part in the way firms make decisions. It can also influence the way that they are managed, how they deliver clients services and how well they respond to change. It will affect how resources are allocated, what reporting mechanisms are needed and the way in which communications and relationships develop.

The 'wrong' structure can inhibit effective management, slow down decision-making and fragment client delivery. As a result, resources appear to be wasted, with a great deal of duplication and a lack of co-ordination. Bottlenecks are common, with some people seeming to have too much to do and others not enough. Communications appear to be disjointed with people not knowing what is happening. Decisions (if taken at all) do not seem to address current needs nor be based on relevant information. As a result, the overall performance of the firm is poor with opportunities missed. Morale is low with people seeing little point in working hard or making suggestions for improvements. Good people leave and a sense of lassitude sets in. People focus on the negative aspects of the firm rather than the positive.

2.8.1 The correct structure?

There is no single correct structure for a professional firm. There is only the correct structure for that particular firm and each firm therefore must work out what that is for itself. This includes both its operational and management structure. It is risky to assume that we know what our operational structure actually is. It is therefore important to carry out a 'Structure Mapping Exercise' as it can tell us a lot about how well people work together and communicate. To complete this exercise, I would suggest that we check any formal organisational structure chart we have against what actually happens in practice. For example, where do people go for help? Which individuals control the unofficial communication channels?

Our operational structure will be dependant on our size, range of client services, geographical locations and style of approach. Our management structure should be tailored to suit our values and could therefore be based on teamwork, consensus or one partner in overall charge of running the firm. Whatever option is chosen, it must support effective communications, manage resource allocation and reporting, and help to co-ordinate and support client services, as well as operational plans and strategies. It must also be flexible enough to respond to changes in demand and service levels. In essence, it must:

1.   facilitate decision-making and implementation,

2.   deliver the resources that the organisation needs,

3.   support consistent and high quality client delivery,

4.   ensure that everyone is clear about their levels of responsibility,

5.   provide the actual and potential skills needed for short-term and long-term success.

Overall it must be able to maintain momentum and facilitate change. It must allow the firm to develop.

2.8.2   Shaping the skill base

Given our dependence on people to provide high quality service, we need to shape our skill base not only to support current services but also to develop future success. To shape the skills base, we need to develop a picture of the skills we will need and the people who will deliver them. To achieve this, we have to complete a Skills Audit mapping out what skills we have, whether they are equally spread throughout the firm, whether they match the demands being made on them, where development is required and whether we need to expand them to support our future shape. From this Audit, we need to build an action plan to support people as well as close any current and future gaps.

Most people want to have interesting jobs and take on more responsibility. Firms need to capitalise on this and as a result, grow their indigenous skill base. They also need to reinforce the commonality and transferability of many core skills (see Chapter 8). Firms need to develop ways of introducing people to business and management skills through, for example, joint ventures with other types of professions.

Succession planning is an important aspect of developing the skill base and should be formalised and not left to chance. However, because of the personal relationships professionals develop with their clients, both the retiring partner and his/her potential successors usually avoid such discussions. However, it is essential to consider succession issues and plan for the transfer of skills and knowledge which otherwise will be lost. Proper discussion of this well in advance of the situation becoming personal is important. As a result, it is worthwhile preparing a Career Profile which identifies career and succession gaps and priorities. This will be developed in more detail in Chapter 8.

It is not always possible to allow everyone to make equity partner as quickly as some people would wish, yet we have established the strategic importance of retaining quality people. Maintaining the motivation of good people can be achieved by having regular discussions with them, some formal career planning and offering secondment opportunities. Such secondments could be for a limited period or one day a week, working with a key client or other professional firm or contact.

It is equally important to check that our leadership and management skills support our growth choice and as our organisation changes its shape and skill base, we must develop these skills to match it.

2.8.3 Does size matter?

Experience and statistics confirm that size is a factor in the success of professional firms, but it is not the only determinant. On average, the larger firms appear to be more profitable per partner, but it is also possible to be equally profitable when smaller. Larger firms (if properly managed) have the potential to be more successful due to their increased resource base. However, smaller firms can also be extremely profitable and often are more able to respond quickly to market opportunities and changes.

The overall message is therefore that size is important – but the size of the firm must follow any development option adopted and must reflect the values of the firm and its people. For example, if the firm decides to adopt a niche strategy, its size and structure should reflect this with a core of high quality professionals providing expert advice in a narrow area of specialism. Other types of work can be referred out to a wider network of firms on a mutual referral basis. If however, the firm decides to be broad based and serve local clients, its structure should reflect this with a few locally known and respected partners, supported by para-professionals doing this typically lower fee type of work. If the firm adopts a high volume, low cost approach, it will require tighter operational controls as it will when working with more skilled and autonomous staff.

2.8.4 Moving through the partnership structure

As mentioned earlier, one of the most significant current trends is that the traditional carrot of partnership no longer assures that young professionals will stay and work hard with the same firm. Not only do they move between firms more readily to gain experience and widen their cvs, they are not so attracted by the risks attached to ownership unless they see potential long-term rewards. Less restrictive career paths need to be developed as more women enter all of the professions.

Most firms cannot make everyone a partner just through passage of time, with the result that there has to be some selection process – formal or informal. Most Partner Profiles (developed in more depth in Chapter 8) contain the same core elements, which include:

- having technical and professional skills, both general and specialised,
- the ability to deliver high quality client service,
- being well regarded with a strong external network of contacts,
- developing good leadership and management skills, and
- a strong understanding of business and financial management.

In addition, there is a growing need to develop professionals with the ability to think innovatively and long term.

Developing a Partner Profile allows younger professionals to work towards achieving that goal, helping to retain their interest in and commitment to the firm as well as providing an objective framework for the partnership to take decisions about who 'makes partner'.

It follows that the next stages down should also be formalised by written profiles i.e. associate partner, senior manager, and department head, so that people are clear about the incremental steps required. It is useful to follow this structuring through the whole firm – office managers, supervisors, para-professionals and support staff. This ensures that people are clear about their roles and responsibilities as well as providing a structure for people to progress through.

Some kind of formal appraisal process is also important as it helps to ensure the objectivity of any assessment of people's performance and contribution to the firm. This is another area where this attempt at structuring could clash with the preferred behaviour of professionals. Professionals feel that only they can be the judge of their competence and as a result, do not behave well when asked to accept the introduction of a formal appraisal process. Great care must be taken to ensure that the policies and standards imposed 'fit' the firm. Any procedures introduced must be tailored to the values of the firm and its style of management.

2.8.5 External structures

It is important also to look at our external structures, in other words, those relationships which we have with other organisations. Any external structure developed by the firm must provide access to additional resources and market information without the need to directly pay for them. To achieve this, some firms have joined formal networks or associations, offering the potential for direct referrals of work and/or clients. Other firms have adopted a less formal approach, referring work to other professionals if the services sought by the client is outwith their area of expertise and/or not profitable for them to undertake. Some 'multi-discipline' associations have been formed with clients being offered a package of support.

Too often partners work in isolation building their individual personal networks and connections. What is of equal importance is that the firm develops some mechanism for capturing information about these external resources and their availability. These mechanisms can include monthly business development reports, which include details of contacts made and an effective, up-to-date and accessible database. We will look more closely at 'knowledge management' in later Chapters.

Conclusions

The Model for Success offers a structure to support the success of our firms. It is based on extensive and applied research into professional firms in the context of their values, professionalism and business success.

Putting in place each Segment allows us to develop effective leadership and management, maximise our use of resources, build relations of value with our clients, make the correct strategic choice and adapt and expand our structure and skill base. Each Segment is important in its own right as it provides practical advice about how to build success and working through the Model allows us to develop the ability to change. It is important to position our firms against each of these five Segments to allow us to identify and implement key priorities and actions.

Key Action Points

1.   first of all, establish effective leadership and management
2.   identify, agree and uphold core values
3.   focus on developing trust
4.   ensure that resources are being used to their maximum
5.   ask our clients why they stay with us
6.   tackle costs with clients up front
7.   make conscious choices about our long-term strategies
8.   check our structure and skills against those choices

Appendix – Business Plan Template

A suggested template for a business plan should include:

Heading 1 Introduction

Heading 2 Where are we now? Ch 2 & 5
- An analysis of the current firm including:
  - Our Values
  - Our Commonality of Purpose
  - Our strengths and weaknesses
  - The services we provide
  - Our people and their expertise
  - Our structure and systems
  - Our current resource level
  - The clients we serve
  - Our direct and indirect competitors
  - Marketplace opportunities
  - Marketplace threats

Heading 3 How well have we performed in the past? Ch 2 & 5
- What we learned from this review (e.g. SWOT)
- As a result, what we will build on
- What we will now change

Heading 4 The current and future marketplace Ch 3 & 7
- The key trends directly affecting us
- Their effect on us and how we will respond

Heading 5 Where do we want to be in the future? Ch 6 & 7
- What we should look like
- What people will be saying about us
- How will we know that we are successful
- Our long-term objectives

Heading 6 How are we going to get there? Ch 2, 5 & 8
- Our short and medium-term objectives
- Our people skills and other resources

- An outline of financial targets
- Our critical success factors
- What changes we need to make and why
- Resource implications (both financial and other)
- Our Action Plan

Heading 7 Financial Projections

3

TACKLING CURRENT CHALLENGES

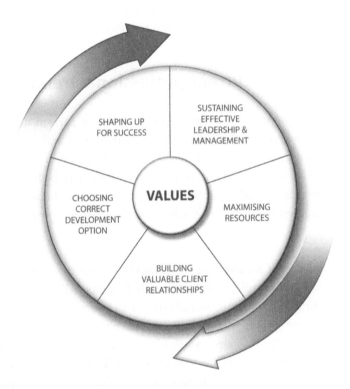

3.1   Introduction

Most of us working in the professional sector feel that the marketplace is putting pressure on us to change the way we deliver client services. In this Chapter, we will analyse these pressures and their relevance to allow us to feel more in control of our future direction and success. We will also review some of the established experts in the field of management, look at what they suggest and identify the elements directly applicable to our areas of concern. Current themes include knowledge management, partnering and emotional robustness. Much of what they offer fits well with professionals and professional firms. As a result, we should be re-assured that we do not need to introduce dramatically new models or ways of working, but merely refine what we currently do to achieve accelerated improvements.

In addition, we will look at the current pressures on professionalism, including what clients now want from us. We will identify ways of tackling this as well as the importance of successfully cross-selling services to our existing clients.

3.2   Review of current professional trends

As discussed in Chapter 2, it is important to consider current market trends, check them against our practices, consider their impact and how we should tackle them. Our competitors will be doing exactly this and may well gain a competitive advantage as a result. Alternatively, they may be handling a time-consuming merger or dealing with a major shift in their client base, and as a result be distracted from noticing what we can take the time to identify as important.

There are a number of recurrent and topical themes for the professional sector at the moment. For example, it seems clear that clients will continue to become more demanding of their professional advisors, expect more for less, question the advice they are given and generally become better informed as consumers. At the time of writing, there continues to be an oversupply of quality professionals in some sectors, less so in others. There is a continuing trend towards externally imposed standards of service. Younger professionals are less attracted by the carrot of a long-term relationship with their employers and more by mobility and short-term rewards. The capital cost of IT requires constant investment, both in time and money, with clients expecting to see their professionals investing heavily and continually in this resource area.

It is worthwhile at this point summarising what we recognise as being the key changes we have experienced in the past 10 years as this summary will allow us to address the concern of many of us that professional life seems to be out of control. It will also allow us to identify some strategic shifts that we must build into our operational responses. Some of these shifts stem from as far back as the difficult property market in the early 1990s, which resulted in a lack of investment in technology and training and others from encroachment by other jurisdictions and professions. Many are the result of an overall increase in consumerism with clients becoming better informed and less impressed with professionals *per se*. External competition and the blurring of professional lines is causing confusion in the marketplace with clients having multiple sources of advice. Information technology and commoditisation of services requires us to re-think how we run our businesses. Overall, the demand for professional services is on the increase, yet at the same time, fee levels have declined in a number of traditional areas of work. As a result, many firms are therefore confusing being busy with being profitable.

3.2.1 Key changes in the past 10 years

1   Clients continue to demand more

Due to the increased consumerism, clients have become much more demanding of their professionals. In addition, decreased levels of market activity in the early 1990s resulted in quality work being in short supply, with too many good professionals chasing a small number of key clients. Clients began to demand 'beauty parades' with professionals being asked to pitch for work. Client loyalty disappeared with client shopping around for the 'best price'. Claims and complaints increased as clients, especially commercial clients, saw an opportunity to hold someone accountable for their losses. The power shifted out of the hands of professionals into the hands of their clients. Despite considerable improvement in our responsiveness to individual clients and accessibility of professionals in general, clients today continue to complain about levels of service and value for money.

2   Erosion of traditional areas of fee income

All of the professions have seen the erosion of traditional areas of fee income. Scale fees have mostly disappeared and areas of work, such as audit and conveyancing, which traditionally paid good fees suffering from a drop in fee levels. This has resulted in firms trying to re-position themselves – either by introducing technology to manage the work more cost-effectively, providing it as a 'loss leader' to attract better paid work in other areas or moving out of the market completely. Most successful are those who now handle this type of work profitably despite the reduced fees.

3   Changes in operational structure

The regional market saw firms of between 10 and 15 partners under the most pressure. They were not large enough to have sufficient resources to invest in the levels of technology, marketing and financial skills being demanded and too large to respond quickly to changes in client demands. At the time of writing, partnership structure continues to be the preferred trading option, with all that implies for funding, decision-making and implementation. Small niche firms were and are still able to show profits per partner equivalent to the largest commercial practices.

Amalgamation and mergers became a common strategic option and continue to be used, especially to support geographical expansion. We are currently seeing the results of tensions within some of those mergers with a significant increase in partner departures, restructuring and de-mergers. The number of small firms has increased, often set up by professionals frustrated by the politics of the larger firms.

4   Blurring of professional lines and external competition

The lines between the professions have become increasingly blurred. Accountants chase work usually provided by lawyers, surveyors and architects compete for the same type of project work, building societies have become banks and banks move out of traditional banking into financial services. With clients more global, other jurisdictions have also started to encroach. External competition is on the increase as professional monopolies are abolished and information technology allowing routine work to become commoditised

5   Good experienced professionals in short supply

Because of the pace of change and increased complexity of professional work, good quality experienced professionals are in short supply. This affects the marketplace in a number of ways. As the 'carrot' of partnership no longer encourages young people to work hard for little return in the short term, many have become disaffected by the long hours now demanded of them. Because of pressures on profitability, they may not receive the 'breadth' of training they used to get. This means that some of them have a narrow focus and limited skills and are not easily re-employable when the demand for services changes. As a result, both they and their firms are adopting a short-term approach to their working relationship.

6   Mobility in the market of partners and teams

Historically, professionals did not move between firms. Indeed, too much movement on a professional's c.v. indicated a lack of stability or an underlying problem with technical ability or overall competence. In recent years, this trend has reversed. As more women enter the professions, career breaks and changes of direction are often required. Headhunting is now common. Partners and whole teams leave firms, sometimes taking 'gardening leave' for a few months, before re-appearing with much publicity in a rival firm. Most partnerships have dealt with significant departures of key groups of people in the past two or three years. This trend is causing major management problems and requires considerable investment in skills and time.

7   The impact of technology and external regulation

The professions have not been alone in seeing technology fundamentally alter the way they work and the skills they require. All professionals have had to become computer-literate. Our daily routine is dominated by e-mails and mobile phones with clients expecting to be able to interact with us instantly. As a result, firms need to invest and keep investing in technology and are totally dependent on having immediate access to skilled IT support.

Most professions are now being subjected to increasing external regulations and controls, imposing administration burdens which most professions feel add little if any, improvement to the quality of client service delivery. As a result of a small number of extreme examples of professional misconduct, it is no longer assumed that professionals can judge their own competence.

8   Reduction in income and lifestyles

Decreasing fees, increased levels of service and longer working hours coupled with an increase in client complaints and claims have led to erosion of job satisfaction. Good professionals are increasingly unhappy about the extent of 'back-covering' required through increased external regulation and the amount of time and energy expended in dealing with non-client work. Professionals value their independence and standing in society, yet many feel this is under threat. Stress is on the increase with its resultant effect on health and family. Many professionals now complain of experiencing pressure to move away from the values and standards they want to adhere to.

9   The structure of partnership

Most professional firms have accepted and continue to accept the need for formal management and a move away from the traditional partnership structure of involving all of the partners in operational decisions. Many have appointed professional managers, restructured into departments or divisions, and ensured they have access to up-to-date financial or business information. Because of rising capital costs, particularly associated with IT investment, the issue of sourcing third party funding is becomingly increasingly important.

10   The pace of change

The pace of change increases exponentially with each decade. The external market continues to cope with the impact of too much information and not enough time, of increasing globalisation and mobility of staff and pressure to reduce costs while at the same time invest in the long term. Most of us complain about the pace of change, yet this is not new. I came across an illuminating quote written about life in 1794:'*Our world was changing and we half understood it. Partly scrabbling to keep up, partly feeling ourselves to be just ahead of a monstrous game in which those who pause are swept away*' (Osborne, 1999 p31). Change is an integral part of life and must be managed as such.

3.2.2   Strategic shifts for the professional sector

This analysis of the ten key changes allows us to determine some key strategic shifts of emphasis applicable to the whole professional service marketplace. These include that we must continually:

1.   add value to our client service delivery, as providing high quality professional services is the minimum that clients now demand,
2.   focus on the profitability of our client services,
3.   find ways to increase our resource base,
4.   develop new ways of delivering and expanding our services,
5.   attract and retain high quality professionals who fit in with our culture and values,
6.   increase our management skills, especially people management,
7.   invest in and train people in technology and manage compliance with external regulations,
8.   seek to achieve a healthy work/life balance and maintain our professionalism,

9. review our trading and operational structures, and
10. accept and become comfortable with a fast pace of change.

It is important therefore not to try to tackle too many initiatives all at the same time. Most of us are encumbered with existing structures, work practices, clients and people. It is essential not to underestimate the limitations these impose in tackling current challenges. As Business Development Partner for my firm, I quite often sat in my office and considered whether I had the energy to push through a development idea that I had – regardless of its merits. I continually meet managing partners who are simply exhausted by the resistance they are encountering from partners and staff to make even the slightest change in the way things are done.

If we all had the luxury of starting up in business anew, we would be able to choose from a variety of responses. People may have worked together before deciding to go out on their own, and as a result, know and are comfortable with each other's values and work practices. They will have the freedom to start from a blank piece of paper when it comes to location of work environment, style of working and even the clients they take on (or take with them). As a result, it is much easier for them to experiment with new ways of working, flexible reward packages for partners and staff, and niche client services. For the rest of us, we have to select key priorities and tackle them one at a time.

In addition, care has to be taken to adopt a response to these shifts which accords with our professional and personal values. For instance, there is little point in deciding to increase our resource base through amalgamation when our people have a core value of autonomy and independence.

3.3 Review of current management experts

Many readers may be cynical about management theories and will identify with the common after-dinner story about management consultants borrowing someone's watch and then charging for telling him or her the time. However, in my view, it is always worthwhile to look at what current management experts are saying. Many professionals tend to consider that the problems they face are specific to them and take too narrow a view of where solutions may lie. Yet professionals like an intellectual challenge and offering them a new management theory allows them to exercise their analytical and critical abilities.

In this section, I have selected people regarded as expert in their field who write on topics which are challenging and exciting. I have included full references to allow further reading into areas of particular interest. In précis, current themes being offered by management experts include that:

1.   our competitive advantage lies in the application of the knowledge we have rather than inert information,
2.   clients and customers want tailored and innovative solutions,
3.   to be successful, we need to be able to 'learn',
4.   organisations need to move away from formal trading structures into collaborative and informal partnerships, and
5.   we need to recognise and accept the role emotions play in our business relationships.

Some of the current themes developed below may not be seen as new or particularly insightful. In my view, this is because professionals have always been knowledge workers and many work in partnering relationships. However, it is important not to disregard commentaries on these issues just because we work in these areas ourselves.

I will move on to look at each of these five themes in more detail.

3.3.1 Knowledge Management – what it means in practice?

As indicated above, it is the accepted view that our competitive advantage lies in our applied knowledge. This has resulted in (or has stemmed from) a great deal being written about knowledge management and the strategic importance of developing knowledge workers (Hammer, 1988; Cortada, 1998). These expert writers argue that our competitive advantage lies in our ability to capture and harness the knowledge that exists in our organisations in such a way that we can all easily access it, develop it and deliver it to our clients. In other words, we need to share what we know, use it and continue to do so. It is important to remember that it is the *application* of knowledge that is important.

In my opinion, none of this is new to professionals, who have always been knowledge workers. Most of our contribution to any business is based on the technical knowledge we carry in our heads and more importantly, our ability to apply that knowledge in practice to meet the needs of our clients. We expect an engineer to use his or her knowledge of structures to build a bridge, which can withstand the strains that will be put on it. We commission architects for their skills in marrying design with what will be practical when built.

It is argued (Hammer, 1988) that knowledge workers differ from process workers in that they are committed to achieving an end result and not simply to completing a series of tasks. They take ownership of projects and responsibility for their own work. Indeed they may resist following established procedures, preferring to use their skills and prior experience to adjust their services to suit the client or particular situation. When projects are changed, they react and respond instinctively.

Most writers agree that trust is the key element in knowledge management (Edvinsson & Malone, 1997; Cohen & Prusak, 2001; Davenport & Prusak, 2000; Pritchard et al, 2000). Trust is an essential element in all long-term relationships and I would argue therefore that knowledge management is therefore based on relationships and not processes. Unfortunately, in my experience, many organisations have missed this fundamental point and have invested a great deal of money in installing a knowledge management computerised system without making sure that their *culture* supports its use.

Edvinsson & Malone (1997) have sought to highlight the importance that knowledge brings to a business by listing intellectual capital as an asset that should be valued on corporate balance sheets. They describe at p11 that *'Intellectual Capital'* is the sum of its human capital (i.e. the knowledge, skills, abilities and attitude of its employees) and its structural capital (i.e. customers, processes and intellectual property).

Success and knowledge are interlinked. Successful businesses attract knowledgeable people as they offer high quality clients and well-resourced work. Knowledgeable people in turn provide high quality services which merit high fees and profile. This implies that knowledge workers and successful client delivery are one and the same. However, many of us know that this may not happen in practice, if we think for example, of academic institutions filled with knowledge workers but not necessarily customer focused. The solution to this issue lies in our interpretation of the phrase *'knowledge workers'*. What we aspire to employ are people who work *with* their knowledge, who apply it in practice, and solve client problems in a practical and timely way.

This consideration of knowledge management has therefore an important practical application for us. It allows us to identify 'knowledgeable people', in other words people who:

- share information and communicate well,
- like helping and show that they care,
- are enthusiastic and energetic,
- inspire trust and build relationships,
- see links and build bridges both internally and externally,
- are respected and technically skilled, and
- see solutions rather than problems.

It can therefore serve as a guide to help in our people selection and development.

In addition, we need to develop ways of capturing our internal knowledge – to devise systems that identify people's expertise and develop ways of sharing it. (Von Krogh et al (eds), 1998 offer a number of interesting examples of these). Too often, knowledge is carried around in people's heads, with the result that we need to discover how to turn what is implicit into explicit.

3.3.2 Innovation – instead of creativity

As considered above, our clients want us to add value to our service delivery. This requires us to think differently about what we do and how we do it and look at ways of introducing innovative practices. In my view, it is important to distinguish between creativity and innovation. In its simplest terms, creativity is about having ideas whilst innovation is about putting the ideas into practice (cf. Barker, 2002 p3).

Research (Plsek, 1997, p10) indicates that innovation is necessary because:

- it is associated with long-term financial success,
- our clients demand it,
- our competitors copy existing products and services,
- investment in new technology requires new ways of working, and

- what used to work in the past does not work any more.

One of the main protagonists of the strategic importance of innovation is Amidon (1997). She argues at p47 that if managers insist that people change, this creates fear in our organisations. In her view, it is much more important to tackle change more indirectly through asking people to be innovative.

In my experience, innovative thinking does not come naturally to professionals. We are trained to be risk adverse, to analyse issues, to identify what might go wrong rather than take an adventurous view and be 'creative'. However, Barker (2002) puts the case at p19 that creative people demonstrate:

1. a high tolerance of ambiguity,
2. a talent for seeking out problems and research,
3. mental mobility,
4. objectivity about their work,
5. self motivation, and
6. a willingness to take risks.

With the exception of number six, all fit neatly into a job description for a good professional. In my view, therefore it would appear that a good professional *can* be innovative as long as we address the risks associated with its use. (We will look later at this issue of managing risks in Chapter 5.)

Another area of particular interest to those who manage professionals on a daily basis is the inter-relationship between innovation and conflict. As we have discussed already, professionals are good at being robust and independent. Leonard & Swap, (1999) argue at p50 that creative abrasion is important to ignite creativity, focusing on a '*clash of ideas – not a clash of people*'. Passion is important and most professionals care about what they do (cf. Hammer 1988, p137). Eisaguirre (2002) also suggests at p261 that conflict should be managed to '*drive creativity and productivity*'.

As indicated at the outset of this section, we need to develop practical innovation, not just abstract creativity. As a result we need people with ideas (divergent thinkers) and people who can turn these ideas into reality (convergent thinkers). This reflects the two aspects to strategic thinking we discussed in Chapter 2 (cf. Reid, 2002, p22).

Again, this review of innovation provides us with insights about our people management and development. We need to encourage professionals to be innovative in their approach to client service delivery, apply their knowledge, debate options and identify solutions. As we result, we need to allow them to learn.

3.3.3 Learning organisations

Successful organisations are able to 'learn' – in other words, are flexible, adaptable and resource effective (Cope, 1998). De Geus (1999) has developed the theme into '*The Living Company*' that is able to adapt: – '*i.e. learn, has its own identity or persona, creates relationships with people inside and out, and develops or evolves over time*' (p32). Learning is also seen as an essential element of leadership, for example, the Janus leader (Chowdhury, 2000 p17) who is able to look both forward and back.

Again, this concept is not new for professionals. All professionals are committed to continuing professional development, of teaching young professionals and helping them develop. Our relationships with fellow professionals and professional bodies last our entire working life. However, in my experience, many professional organisations do not seem to be able to 'learn'. This may be caused by rigidity of structure with individual departments failing to communicate with or support each other. It may be caused by a refusal to share information between professionals. Learning implies listening, allowing mistakes and responding.

In my opinion, the best professional firms are 'learning' organisations but there are many who operate a 'blame' culture. Corrective action is therefore required to eradicate such a culture before both the organisation and its people are able to learn. This theme therefore overlaps with the partnering theme developed below in that it places considerable emphasis on a supportive culture, values, trust and building long-term relationships.

3.3.4 Partnering – what we all should be doing?

In recent years, we have heard a great deal about the need to work in strategic partnership with other people. We heard about partnerships between the private and public sector, about partnering in the construction of new hospitals and schools; about the private heath care sector working with the public; and about global partnerships creating dominant accountancy and legal firms. Businesses are urged to form partnerships with their suppliers and with their customers. Leaders are encouraged to develop partnering relationships, both internally and externally (Segil et al, 2003). Books about mergers (e.g. Marks & Mirvis, 1998) emphasise the essential importance of shared values and cultures. Strategic alliances are very much in vogue as a strategic development route (Cauley de la Sierra, 1995; Doz & Hamel, 1998). Similarly 'boundaryless' and 'virtual organisations' (Ashkenas et al, 1995) are being encouraged as they provide us with the opportunity to expand our geographical reach and resource base. Collaboration is important for all organisations, both internally, as experts encourage us to focus on communicating and working in a collegiate way (Schrage, 1989) and externally, as we seek client feedback and find ways to build loyalty (Maister, 2000).

Many professionals feel that the word 'partnering' has been overused in recent years. In many cases the word is used without an understanding of what 'partnership' implies. For example, in the construction industry, the reality of the relationship being formed is the direct opposite of what we would traditionally consider to be a 'partnership' i.e. a relationship based on trust, shared aspirations and culture.

It is also important to look at 'partnering' and its relationship to leadership and coaching (Segil et al, 2003). Most management experts (e.g. Hammer, 1988 p117) focus on the need for leaders to work collaboratively with their people – to persuade them to commit to their organisations which need their energy, enthusiasm and creativity to develop and deliver high quality client services and products. As a result, they need to become motivational coaches rather than dictators (Bolt, 2000).

Values also come up again and again in any consideration of partnerships (Marks & Mirvis, 1998; Segil et al, 2003 p243). Edvinsson (2002) highlights this by arguing that *'the more networked and partnership oriented the enterprise becomes, the more essential is the need for explicit values'* (p136). As we developed in Chapter 2, without common and core values, relationships cannot function. They provide the basis of our culture, our communications and our understanding of each other. With common core values, a lot of our understanding of each other can be taken on trust.

This leads us neatly on to the next topical area – emotions.

3.3.5 Emotional Intelligence

To most people, it is obvious that emotional robustness is an essential part of professional success as successful firms are based on their relationships with people. In addition, emotional resilience is essential in managing change. Few of us have the luxury of controlling the marketplace in which we operate. As a result, we need to be comfortable with ambiguity and uncertainty. As the speed of change increases, we need to make decisions quicker and be more flexible.

Yet, emotions have traditionally been disregarded in the business environment. Business issues tended to focus around analysis, financial information and audit trails. Strategic tools offered structures to analyse, consider and make business decisions based on logical and rational choices. More recently, however, emotions have become much more accepted with intuition, gut feelings and the effect of people's behaviour now seen as influencing business performance and operational success. Kets de Vries (2001) takes up this point, suggesting that *'crucial sub-skills… are listening actively, picking up on nonverbal communication and keying into the wide spectrum of emotions'* (p32).

Professionals are used to working under pressure to make decisions quickly. Nicholson (2000) argues that our human survival responses, such as making snap judgements and competitiveness, are so strong that we cannot override or disregard them. Mintzberg offers that *'our best managers and leaders operating in our rapidly changing and extremely complex environment do so by relying on instinct'* (Cooper & Sawaf, 1997 p233). Clients choose us because of our accurate perception and empathy (Nicou et al, 1994) and because they like us as people (Maister, 1997 & 2000). Cooper & Sawaf (1997 p54) describe this as *'the feeling of connection'.*

We established in Chapter 1 that professionals are not easy to manage. Many partners are successful because of their strength of personality. Managers working with professionals confirm to me that a great deal of their time and energy is spent managing behavioural issues and relationships. As a result, we simply cannot afford to disregard the effect of emotions and resultant behaviours. Goleman (1998) has developed the concept of *'emotional intelligence'* as a necessary attribute describing it as exhibiting *'internal qualities such as resilience, optimism and adaptability'* (p11). Cooper & Sawaf (1997, p196) argue that emotions *'are integral to values such as trust, integrity, empathy, resilience and credibility i.e. our ability to build and sustain relationships and for leadership'.* This brings us full circle back to our definition of professionalism and the emphasis that professionals put on their values.

Understanding of this issue helps us with our people management and development. We need to look for more than technical competence and develop emotionally balanced people with 'softer skills', such as self-awareness, understanding of others, tolerance and integrity. This links into our discussion about innovation. It is also a crucial element of our ability to perform as professionals. We need resilience and courage to deal with difficult issues and stand our ground when faced with pressure to back down. Most of us work in highly charged and stressful situations on a daily and routine basis. We have to make 'grey' decisions, often quickly and with a great deal of emotionally charged information. We have to learn to rely on our own judgement and not to expect recognition or thanks for what we do. When we get it right, clients argue that that is what they pay us to do. When we get it wrong, there are often severe and serious consequences.

3.4   Where is professionalism going?

As outlined above, many management experts are advocating a move towards increased professionalism – of the importance of values, knowledge management, emotional integrity and the like. At the same time, those of us working in the professional environment feel that our professionalism is under threat. We are experiencing an apparent lack of trust from government with increasing external regulation and independent scrutiny, with clients becoming more and more demanding and consumer orientated, and colleagues willing to move around much more. As a result, we are now faced with managing a number of inherent dichotomies. These include:

- how do we maintain our independence and regulate ourselves to meet external standards?
- how do we serve our clients interests and protect ourselves from spurious claims?
- how do we invest in training younger members of our profession and ensure that our own career is not jeopardised as a result of passing on our skills?

In my view, the answers lie in our continued commitment to professionalism.

The essence of professionalism continues to be to serve the public regardless of self interest, to provide a collegiate environment where people share information and to maintain a high quality standard of service. We allow people to learn from and lean on each other. We invest in the long-term future of our profession. We do not *'take'* from our clients, our colleagues, our staff or our trainees, or adopt a short-term view of how much we can earn or get away with.

I confess that I am worried about the future of professionalism. I am not sure whether many of you reading the paragraph above would agree that the behaviour of some current professional firms and professionals reflects what I have written about the essence of professionalism. Some firms seem to be adopting a short-term, aggressive approach to their internal culture and external client service delivery. Senior people appear to be stressed, working long hours and having little work-life balance. Junior and support staff are doing their best with limited training and support. As an outsider, I often observe extreme behaviour, which for those people working in the firm has become 'normal'. This results in younger people copying such behaviour as they think that that is what has made that person 'successful'. However, what may have started out as professional attributes, such as being intellectually robust, may under pressure of fee generation, workload and time demands, have become abrasiveness, arrogance and self-centred rudeness. One of the knock-on effects of this short-term approach is increased mobility in the job marketplace. We will look at the implications of this and how to manage it in Chapter 8.

3.5   What do professionals want?

Professionals want what most people want – to work in a supportive environment, to feel valued and give value in return.

When starting out on their career, they want to learn, to do their best and when they make mistakes, be supported. They want to work with more senior people who will willingly share their knowledge and experience. They want to incrementally take on more responsibility, and work on interesting and challenging assignments. They want people to invest in them, help to build their skills and when they move to another role, to have 'transferable' skills. In other words, they are looking for good leadership from their employers.

Senior people often argue with me that younger professionals are too arrogant, want to 'run before they can walk', have too high expectations of their own abilities and are not willing to take criticism. They feel they are not prepared to do basic level work. Conversely, young professionals argue that they are often asked to do administrative work, are blamed for problems not of their making and are given work to do without adequate instruction. Like most arguments, the answer lies somewhere in the middle. Young professionals have skills and knowledge which may be under-utilised but lack an understanding of their application. Senior professionals can be abrupt and impatient, assume that people can read their minds and know what they want them to do without explanation.

What most professionals want is to reflect their values. True professionalism lies in our ability to use our skills and expertise to help people, whether clients or colleagues. We want to be able to build our abilities by learning and working in a supportive environment. We want to be respected by the people we work with and for. We want to feel 'valued' and 'rewarded' for what we do.

3.6   What do clients want?

My experience of listening to clients continues to highlight the lack of understanding that exists between professionals and their clients. Clients do not know what individual professions do. For example, what is a forensic audit? What takes so much time in a house sale? What is the difference between a building and a quantity surveyor? Many professional firms are beginning to appreciate this and concentrate in their web sites, brochures and the like on giving basic information about services, highlighting the benefits they bring to clients rather than technical details (see Chapter 6). However, as we have already discussed, many firms tend to make assumptions about what their clients want, rather than asking the clients directly. Some firms have identified key clients and appointed Client Relation Partners, but many continue to be 'scared' to approach clients for fear of hearing bad news. Yet, surely if the potential for bad news exists is it not preferable to find this out and address it rather than risk losing an important client?

Clients want to feel supported by their professionals, recognised for their individuality and given value for money. I appreciate that these elements are vague and subjective, but surely that is the point of providing a service. As argued in Chapter 2, the quality of our services is judged by the end-user (i.e. our clients) and not by us as the service provider. For instance, only you can judge whether I have delivered a quality product by how useful you have found this book.

Similarly, caring about what we do is an essential part of being a professional. Recognising what each client wants and tailoring our approach is what makes our job exciting and varied. Providing value for money does not imply providing a cheap job, as good clients, in my experience, will pay what they perceive as a fair price for a quality service.

Ironically, therefore, both clients and their professionals want the same thing. Both want to work with people they can relate to, who listen to them and respect their views, and who work *with them*. Professionals complain about a lack of client loyalty; yet clients complain about a lack of professional loyalty. I accept that up to the late 1980s, clients were too much in awe of their professionals and many professionals charged a lot of money for a poor level and quality of service. In the 1990s, the power shifted to our clients who became much more critical of their professionals and their service, 'shopping' around for the best price. Perhaps the time has come for the power to be equally split – with clients and professionals both benefiting from the relationship.

3.7   The importance of cross selling

This brings me to one of the major challenges for professional service firms – the importance of *implementing* successful cross selling.

Just about every professional service Business Plan I see or help to develop talks about the strategic importance of cross-selling services to new and existing clients. Yet, there are very few firms who actually achieve it. The reasons for this are often inter-related. The culture of the firm may reinforce the importance of hoarding clients to ensure that individual or departmental targets are met and its reward mechanism may reflect this. Partners may be ignorant about the range of services available in other departments. They may be worried about damaging their own relationship with particular clients if they refer them across. They may be uncomfortable with the concept of 'selling'. We will develop these themes in more detail in Chapter 6.

However, it is important to appreciate that in fact, cross selling is not a strategic option – it is an operational necessity! Clients rarely present us with one specialised problem. For example, if they want to retain us to manage a property development for them, they want us to manage (formally or informally) the other professionals involved. If the development contract runs into difficulties, they do not want to be sent away to find another expert to advise them on it – they want *us* to help them through it. However, if we refer them on to someone else inside our firm, clients do *not* want to have to start again to develop a relationship with that new person or department. Clients are able to tell me numerous stories about the difficulties they have experienced through 'cross selling'. Most have had to go through the whole process of educating the new person with their background and basic information. Their names are often spelled incorrectly and their personal details not understood.

If we are not able to successfully achieve cross-selling of our services, then we are facing a major problem. If people cannot work together to service existing clients with existing services, then our firm will struggle both in the short and long term. In the current marketplace, there are too few quality clients and an oversupply of apparently quality professional firms. Only when we have mastered cross selling is it possible to look at other strategic options as having a foundation built of quality service and quality clients underpins all of these.

3.8   Dichotomies of managing continuous change

We have reviewed the views of management experts about the need to become more innovative and allow our people to learn, at the same time as market trends are forcing us to work to external standards and apply good risk management to control the advice we give. In addition, we have clients who have become more critical and demanding, we operate in a market where people are much more mobile, yet at the same time, we have to build our skill base and expertise and develop our professional image and reputation. As a result, we must be able to manage a series of contradictions – of conducting a balancing act between one pressure and another. At operational level, there are four inherent dichotomies in tackling the challenges we have outlined above:

1.   we need to be able to attract and retain the best people and manage them
2.   we need to deliver exceptional service and be risk and cost effective

3.   we need to be client responsive and have control over our lives, and

4.   we need to be careful in the way that we work and be innovative.

It is important to accept and manage these contradictions, rather than complain about them. Resolving these is therefore part of the day-to-day management we face and will lead to long-term success. As a result, we need to build all four elements into everything we do. For example, we need to focus on recruiting people who fit with our core values, because they will know how to behave lessening the need for formal management of them. We need to focus on delivering exceptional service, tailored to what our clients' value and as a result, we will be less likely to face complaints and claims. Responding to what our clients want from us allows us to spend time and energy doing what they value, rather than wasting time on non-profitable aspects of our services. When our clients see value in what we do, they will be less likely to complain, allowing us to have the time and energy to do the job well and quickly.

In theory we should be comfortable with problem-solving as that is what clients pay us to do. However, this is turn creates another tension. Professionals like to see successful resolutions or completions of projects and deals and then move onto the next challenge or piece of client work. We do not like loose ends or unfinished files. Yet to be a successful manager of a professional firm, we need to become comfortable with never seeming to see satisfactory ends to our work. We are often blamed for problems not of our making, and may spend hours dealing with difficult people with little personal recognition of our efforts and limited job satisfaction in the traditional sense of seeing a piece of technical work well done. Indeed, success for practice managers will result in the absence of problems, the absence of fire-fighting, the absence of poor behaviour from key players in the firm. As a result, unless undertaking a major expansion or a merger, there will be little tangible evidence of our skills. If things are going well, people assume that is what happened naturally. If things are not going well, this will laid at our door. Not only do we need to become comfortable with this lack of recognition and tangible results, we need also to become comfortable with inherent tensions. This takes considerable skill including having the ability to influence other people without necessarily having direct authority over them as well as limitless patience.

What is essential is our ability to develop the skills to manage this difficult chameleon called a professional service firm. It often appears to change shape before our eyes, especially as the mood of the work environment is determined by the mood of its people.

The attributes necessary to manage continuous change may seem obvious. They include:

- patience and tolerance,
- resilience and tenacity,
- not to be dependent on external recognition of achievements,
- integrity and the ability to inspire trust, and
- optimism and adaptability.

And we need to develop a culture where change is the norm.

As explained in Chapter 2, the Model for Success is built around the need to start the wheel turning and initiate movement. It is important to begin with achieving some small success which directly impact on people and their work environment, as once people learn to accept change as a positive experience, they are much more likely to take bigger steps. Too much change too quickly will unsettle people and make them dig in their heels and resist it. However, once change starts and is seen to benefit everyone, it is much easier to sustain that movement. Anyone who has studied physics knows the importance of momentum. And this is where the attributes of patience, tolerance and resilience are vital.

3.9   Role of the outsider and objectivity

By now some of you may well be feeling overwhelmed by the challenges outlined above. That is not my intention. I prefer to take the view that rather than worry about everything and anything, it is preferable to work out what is bothering us and identify our priorities.

We need to work out what elements are important to us and what are not. Some of us may be managing a successful firm with a solid and loyal client base and stable personnel. Some may be running a niche practice that is well known and respected with a tight network of quality work and referrals. Some people may have set up a new firm recently and are working with people and handpicked clients. Some of us however, may not have these advantages and instead feel we are drowning in competing demands and resource conflicts. As a result, we are looking for answers about where best to put our time and energy, what should be given priority and what should be disregarded.

I know this will sound like what most external consultants will say, but it is much easier for an outsider to identify what these priorities are. Outsiders have the benefit of objectivity, are independent of 'past baggage' and issues, have experience of other firms, examples of good and bad practice and will be seen as independent from any particular cabal or fiefdom. As a result, it is often easier for people to talk to and be honest with them.

In my experience, for any major project, an outsider is essential, even for a limited time. At the outset, there may be the need to canvass opinion or ascertain what is happening, internally or externally. There may be a need for discussion of sensitive or difficult issues and having an external facilitator in attendance at formal sessions makes people behave better. It is much easier for that person to play 'devil's advocate' and raise issues that need to be aired and resolved. Outsiders also bring with them their own external expertise and objectivity.

Once a project is agreed on, additional resources and skills may well be needed. Operational people may already be stretched. They may never have tackled this type of project before and do not know where or how to start. An extra pair of hands is therefore invaluable in getting the project implemented in a feasible and sensible timescale. Externals are often brought in only at the planning stage, on the assumption that the resulting Action Plan can be implemented in-house. People then get distracted, the Action Plan falls down the priority list and all the time, energy and money that went into the initial stage is wasted. As a result, it is usually better to keep the external in place, even as project manager to see some of the Action Plan through. It also encourages the consultant to facilitate a Plan that is actually achievable.

The recurring theme of this book is the importance of implementing change – not just talking about doing it. As we have already discussed, professionals are trained to analyse and debate. Externals can help to focus this analysis on finding solutions, rather than identifying problems. The challenges of the marketplace are thrown at all of us. Some firms will catch them, analyse them, work out which are significant and then respond to them. Others will duck them, hide their heads in the sand and hope that things will get better without any direct action on their part. Success lies in our ability to respond to change, not run away from it.

Conclusions

Current professional and market trends are putting us under pressure to change. It is essential to analyse them and what they mean for our firm in particular. Some can be discounted and as a result, ignored. Some are significant and need to be responded to.

Current management experts offer theories about marketplace shifts. Most elements, such as knowledge management, learning and partnering are familiar to professional firms. Innovation and emotional intelligence have to be put into context and managed accordingly.

Professionals and clients want the same outcome – to work with people they trust and value. Cross selling our services is an essential element in building our firms and our client relationships. Change is continuous and unavoidable. We need to successfully manage a range of dichotomies, including delivering exceptional services cost effectively. Outsiders can help us achieve that.

Key Action Points

1. manage our response to professional and marketplace changes
2. select and tackle key priorities
3. keep up to date with current management theories
4. put them into practice in the context of professionalism
5. ensure that our people and our clients feel valued
6. implement effective cross selling
7. accept the inherent dichotomy of managing change
8. use outsiders to remain objective and help get things done

4

SUSTAINING EFFECTIVE LEADERSHIP AND MANAGEMENT

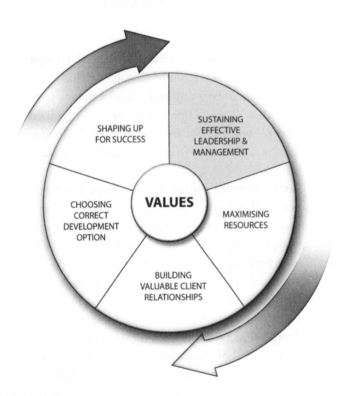

4.1   Introduction

This Chapter focuses on sustaining effective leadership and management. In Chapter 2, we established its importance in implementing the Model for Success and considered the impact of values and the need for trust. In this Chapter, we will identify its individual elements, and the steps required to put these in place.

Most professional firms now accept the importance of management in the way that their businesses are run. Some firms have even successfully implemented the concept within their practices. Others, however, continue to pay lip service to it, often recruiting experienced commercial managers who they then disregard and frustrate. Some have taken the option of moving away from partnership structure in an attempt to become more 'commercial' and now struggle with managing and motivating their professionals. Others have entered into joint ventures or amalgamations and lack the ability to manage the increased resource base that has been created. Sustaining effective leadership and management skills is therefore an operational necessity.

4.2   What makes a good leader or manager?

By now, we can agree that managing professionals, in whatever structure, is not easy. Most professionals cannot be motivated solely by money. Job satisfaction and quality work and clients will always be vitally important to them. Their values and working with people who honour these, continue to be their key drivers and, as illustrated in Chapter 2, the means of managing and motivating them.

Professionals will only allow themselves to be managed and led by people they trust. I use the phrase *'allow themselves'* deliberately because in my experience, professionals will rarely do what they are told. They may agree to follow general principles and an overall approach, but they will never slavishly follow rules and processes. This is both their strength and their weakness. Their strength lies in their ability to question, challenge, analyse and probe until they devise the best course of action and develop a solution that draws on all their abilities and skills. Their weakness lies in their resistance to doing anything by rote, which makes formal management of them difficult, including delegation and risk assessment. It also means that they often exhaust themselves doing routine tasks, rather than concentrating on where their unique skills and expertise can add value to their client delivery. Good leaders and managers have to be able to build on these strengths and tackle the weaknesses.

As argued in Chapter 2, I believe that leadership and management are inseparable. In addition, professionals as they develop through their own career are expected to bring on and teach younger professionals the *'tools of their trade'*. All of this requires the ability to coach and mentor people, rather than tell people what to do. In my experience, the skills of coaching, leadership and management are one and the same. For example, all require considerable skills in listening and motivation. As a result, we can develop a composite description of the attributes required to be a good leader *and* manager of a professional service firm. These include the ability to:

1.   inspire trust and build relationships,
2.   influence people without the use of direct authority,
3.   deal with the impact of behaviour,
4.   tackle conflict constructively,
5.   communicate effectively and listen actively, and
6.   solve problems and achieve long-term solutions.

4.3   Inspire trust and build relationships

In my view, the most important element of leadership and management is the ability to inspire trust. It is also the most intangible of skills and almost impossible to teach. People are either trusted or they are not, usually for reasons we cannot define.

The word 'trust' is often used in an emotive context. For example, we say:

*   *'I can't trust him to be there when I need him',*
*   *'I don't trust her even when she agrees with me',*
*   *'I wouldn't trust him as far as I could throw him',* and/or
*   *'I don't trust what she says behind my back'.*

All these phrases come back to one underlying thing – that for one reason or another, we do not want to work with that individual. Trust is therefore an essential element in our ability to build relationships.

How do we know we do not trust a person? Sometimes we have clear evidence of a person going back on his or her word, but more often we do not have anything specific to rely on. It may be a nuance within a meeting where the person does not say something that we expected. It may be a lack of direct eye contact or it may be just a feeling.

We will look at working with clients we trust in Chapter 6. In this Chapter however, we will focus on developing internal trust. Quite apart from the financial issues for those of us working in an unlimited liability partnership, our reputation, image and future are all interrelated with the people we work with. Especially important these days, trust will allow us to work with people who are geographically remote from us, who we do not see regularly and/or may operate in different cultures and backgrounds. Professionals make judgements about each other based on who they trained with and who they have worked with in the past. We can all think of situations where decent professionals have carried the stigma for years of one 'bad' partner or colleague. Even where they had no direct contact or control over what happened, there is an implication that they *should have seen something was wrong* or *should have sensed that he or she was dangerous*.

How can we establish trust and build relationships?

4.3.1 Follow our instincts

First of all we need to work with people we feel we can trust. Often this will be based on our instincts backed up with our knowledge of their professional track record and feedback we have received from people they have worked with in the past. If from the outset, our instincts tell us that we do not trust that person, we must pay attention to what they are saying. A lot of our ability to trust is based on past experience. If we are unsure about someone, we will need to tread carefully and find out more about their background. To achieve this, we need to ask someone whose judgement we do trust what they know about that person and what they would recommend.

4.3.2 Develop and use shared values

Secondly, we need to establish and articulate some shared values. We looked at the importance of values for professionals in detail in Chapter 2. We also looked at the impact value conflicts have on our organisations, professionalism and health. I cannot emphasise too much the importance of generating a list of shared values within our organisations.

I can best illustrate this point through a recent client project. One part of the firm was very profitable, another was not. Strong personalities existed on both sides. Management consultants had been brought in and unfortunately, tempers had flared without any constructive outcome. I was asked in to see if the partnership could be saved. The aggressive partners were not at all sorry that harsh words had been exchanged whilst the quieter ones dreaded the next formal Partners' meeting. Yet, when I met the partners individually, it was clear to me that they all were committed to the firm and its reputation. What I had to do was get them to realise this. In each individual session, I worked hard to gain their confidence and commitment to follow my lead at their next formal meeting.

People arrived for the meeting looking tense. They talked to me, but not with each other. There was little direct eye contact and the atmosphere was strained. The quieter partners were looking pale and withdrawn. The aggressive ones seemed ready to spring to the attack. I presented a list of values that I had collated from my discussions with them and from their brochures and web site and asked them to select the ten most important to them personally. After a short discussion, we had seven values that everyone had voted for. The relief was tangible. The quieter partners looked visibly relieved. The aggressive ones appeared surprised and started to look round the table at their partners with new respect. In the same meeting, we were able to agree the core aims of the business for the future and a Business Plan. A year later, they were working well together and had successfully implemented a considerable part of their Plan.

4.3.3 Keep using and reinforcing them

Once our common values are established, they have to be *used* as they are the basis of *building* relationships. They must be seen to be applied in practice. They should be referred to in staff recruitment, performance reviews, client presentations and web sites – and followed through and acted upon. Leaders and managers should include them in all internal communications, such as the headings of all meeting agendas and should apply them in their behaviour. For example, if we have a value of 'integrity', then people should behave with openness and honesty. We must show tangible examples of their application in practice. If, for example, we value 'team work', our reward and bonus structure should reflect that.

Trust and relationships are fragile. They can be amazingly strong, allowing people to work well together even when they are geographically apart. They can also be quickly damaged, by something seemingly minor or inconsequential. As a result, it is essential not to do anything that undermines our trust or our core values. We must:

- act with integrity and honesty,
- treat people fairly and consistently,
- have resilience and patience, and
- educate people about themselves and ourselves.

Overall, we need to focus on building long-term relationships based on mutual respect and understanding. We also need to be able to influence people without them feeling that we are imposing our authority on them.

4.4   Influencing without authority

A key skill for leaders and managers working with professionals is therefore the ability to influence them without necessarily having direct authority over them, particularly in professional partnerships. Even where we have direct authority, in my opinion, it is important to *persuade* people rather than *tell* them. Given the power professionals have to influence other people's behaviour we must be able to bring them 'on side'. Often and understandably, managers complain about the 'unmanageability' of their professionals rather than trying to harness their strengths i.e. their intellect, commitment and high standards of integrity. As always with professionals, we need to tap into agreed common values and gain their positive agreement and commitment. Partnerships are particularly susceptible to the power of influence. Quite often they have no formal organisational structure and even when they do, the power of some people can outweigh their formal position in the firm. People may exert influence sometimes by the depth of their client base or capital base, by age or seniority and most often, by the sheer strength of their personality.

In my experience, it is much better to involve influential people in the decision-making process, as they will then be more willing to implement what has been agreed. As a result, professionals need to be managed subtly. We need to be able to build relationships with the key influencers within our organisations in such a way that we can use them to help us rather than have them work against us. Influencing is therefore an essential part of both decision making and more importantly, the implementation of decisions. Good influencers understand the importance of allowing both sides to win and are able to read the dynamics of their organisations. The best influencers resemble good chess players, in that they think strategically and long-term, and are able to remember the interaction of relationships. They appreciate the importance of losing 'a pawn' to win a longer-term advantage. So how do we go about influencing people?

4.4.1 Be clear about what we want to achieve

First of all, the ability to influence people assumes that we have an overall aim in mind or something that we need to achieve. As a result, we need to be clear about what decisions need to be made and even more importantly, what decisions need to be implemented. Too often people concentrate on the first and forget the second. It is important to formally document and promulgate what we want to achieve so that there can be no miscommunication or misunderstanding. We also need to think beyond the short term. All too often people focus on winning the battle and lose the war. There will be situations when tactical choices have to be made, when what appears to be a compromise can pay real dividends in the long term.

4.4.2 Identify and influence the influencers

Once we are clear about what we want to achieve, we need to map out our organisations. It is useful to draw a formal Relationship Map, to show the connections that exist between people. We need to identify the key influencers, in other words, the individuals (or departments) who:

- control the flow of information,
- add to or supplement what is being said,
- influence how people behave,
- affect how people respond, and/or
- people go to for advice, guidance and support.

We must not assume that it will only be the most senior people we have to be concerned with. In many cases, there will be a key individual (or role), such as the person holding the purse strings or other resources that we must influence if we are to succeed. This mapping exercise will produce some interesting gatekeepers and barriers that are the causes of poor or ill-informed communication, and will help to illustrate why things do and do not happen. We must work to keep the gates open and find ways around or over the barriers. Once we have identified the influencers, we need to ensure that we have a positive relationship or links with them.

It is important to continue to think of influencing as a web of connections, mapping it out to ensure that we have no gaps or breaks. Our ultimate aim is to develop a trusting relationship with all of these people. The best way to do that is to listen to their concerns and then, as quickly as we can, show that we can do something to help them. We need to begin to build mutual understanding, so that they move from feeling isolated to being part of the influencing circle. In my experience, it is much easier to manage them from within as this forces them to take responsibility for the practical implications of their demands. As always, the key objective is to agree some common values and aims. This is often the rationale behind formal business planning – that its process allows all interested parties to better understand each other as well as gain an appreciation that resources are not finite and that compromises may be required. It is essential to agree some common ground, which can be used as a frame of reference for future discussions and debates. It is important to agree the key elements of what we *all* want to achieve i.e. increased profits, better use of resources, and/or improved client care. There are some extreme situations where there is so much 'past baggage' and resentment that it is impossible for anyone *within* the organisation to raise the topic as everyone is perceived as having his or her own agenda. In those circumstances, an external facilitator is required, who is seen to be independent and without any predetermined point of view.

Managing professionals requires the skills of a parliamentary lobbyist – knowing who to influence and when. Influencing skills to be successful have to be subtle. They include empathy, the ability to listen, to communicate well and directly, and build long-term relationships. This takes us on to the next area of importance where leadership and management skills are vital – the vexed issue of behaviour.

4.5   The impact of behaviour

We discussed in Chapter 2 the impact that the behaviour of professionals can have on their organisations and other people. Professionals have a powerful effect on other people and how they respond. We can all think of firms who have developed their own particular identity – unpleasant and unhelpful, commercially astute, or gentlemanly and old fashioned. People within our firms become comfortable with behaving in a certain way and copy it themselves. People, who are not comfortable, simply leave.

Partners, in particular, must be wary of this as they set the standard of behaviour of the firm. If they adopt a confrontational style with each other, their staff will mirror that in their behaviour. Because they have become so used to conflict, they may not be aware of how uncomfortable it can make other people. Some people hate conflict of any sort and will leave the firm, rather than work under that kind of pressure. More worryingly, when conflict becomes the norm, our whole attitude to work and relationships adopts a similar stance, often resulting in stress and health problems.

Regardless of how confrontational a situation is, there is no excuse for belittling behaviour or personal ridicule. If people have a significant concern this should be aired directly with the people concerned and not talked about behind their backs. Standards of behaviour must be set by the partners in particular.

Because of the way that professionals are trained – often studying formally in a closed group for four or more years. Working in a narrow technical environment under a more experienced professional, we tend to adopt similar behaviour styles. As a result, we often become unaware of the impact of our behaviour on 'outsiders' and as a result, appear arrogant and remote.

The arrogance of professionals continues to astound non-professionals. One example I heard recently was about a highly regarded paediatric surgeon, who having successfully completed a difficult operation on a child, came out of theatre to reassure the anxious parents by telling them that 'he'll be fine'. The only issue was that 'he' was in fact a 'she'. The surgeon had paid so little attention to the individuality of the child that he had failed to remember what sex it was.

Accordingly, we must define the behaviour we regard as acceptable within our organisations and that supports the values we have agreed. This could include expecting people to take responsibility for themselves and their own work, being willing to learn and allowing others to learn and work collaboratively. A written Behaviour Policy Statement is worth developing. This could include:

- treating people with dignity and mutual respect,
- commitment to equal opportunities,
- a code of conduct on sexual harassment and victimisation,
- some definitions of bullying, and/or
- support on stress management and counselling.

If we ascribe to values of integrity and mutual respect, people must behave in that manner. Nothing is more likely to demotivate people than to promulgate a list of values or 'Commonality of Purpose' which bears no relationship to how people behave in reality. Unacceptable behaviour must therefore be addressed. Managers and leaders must tackle the offenders face to face. Just because they are partners, important rainmakers or fee earners, they should not be allowed to behave badly. In my opinion, there is no excuse for sexist, racist or any kind of bigotry.

4.5.1 Reward good behaviour

The impact of good behaviour on the organisation can be powerful as illustrated by Table 4.5.1. Externally the firm will have a good image and reputation, resulting in ease of recruiting quality people, referrals and repeat business. Organisationally, people will work well together based on mutual trust and resources will be used effectively. People will be keen to learn and develop new skills. With people behaving in the same way to each other and clients, service delivery will be consistent across the firm (see Chapter 6) which results in high client satisfaction. Internally and personally, people will know that *'they fit in'* in the firm, will be committed to it and see a future for themselves. They will *'go the extra mile'* for clients, feeling energised, creative and valued. Privately, they will be well balanced and healthy.

It is essential therefore to reward good behaviour. This can be done in a number of ways, including recognising it formally in job descriptions, appraisals, mentoring, client feedback and project debriefs. It must also be done informally and routinely, with people thanking each other for helping and putting in an extra effort, by department meetings highlighting client successes and passing on clients' praise for a job well done.

However, it is equally important not to re-inforce bad behaviour by hoping that people will not notice if someone is behaving in an unacceptable way. It must be tackled in a way that reduces rather than increases the level of conflict.

Table 4.5.1 Good Behaviour Matrix

	Internal Impact	External Impact
Organisational	ORGANISATIONAL Excellent communications Effective team working Resources used well People develop and learn quickly Consistent service delivery High client satisfaction	PROFESSIONAL Good publicity and awards Excellent reputation Success in recruiting good people Referral work and repeat business
Individual	PERSONAL Strong career paths High quality client work Sharing and learning, energy and commitment, mutual support	PRIVATE Balance between work and private life Good health and well-being

4.5.2 Deal with bad behaviour

If unacceptable behaviour is allowed to happen without challenge, it will have both a direct and indirect effect. It directly damages the recipient, resulting in people leaving, employment tribunals and bad publicity. It also causes health and stress-related problems for everyone involved – the recipient, the people causing the problem and their managers. It also creates a spiral of demotivation. Good people who are striving to mitigate the effects of bad behaviour will become disaffected. Others will become cynical of the organisation and its leadership with dealing with bad behaviour providing a litmus test of management. When they see senior people unable or unwilling to tackle this very tangible challenge of leadership, it provides them with demonstrable illustrations of the weakness of management. It allows them to say *'nothing will ever change here, so what is the point in supporting the firm?'* and undermine any attempt to introduce change on whatever topic.

Bad behaviour can have a devastating effect on the organisation, externally and internally (see Table 4.5.2). Externally, it will be the recipient of bad publicity, industry gossip and have a poor professional reputation with the result that

Table 4.5.2 Bad Behaviour Matrix

	Internal Impact	External Impact
Organisational	ORGANISATIONAL Time taken up dealing with personnel issues Poor communications Rumours and gossip Tensions and fiefdoms Staff turnover and absenteeism Managers and leaders called into question	PROFESSIONAL Bad publicity Poor reputation Difficulty in recruiting good people Claims and complaints Industrial tribunals
Individual	PERSONAL Time tied up in internal relationship issues Increased cynicism Good people becoming disaffected	PRIVATE Health and stress related problems for all involved

quality people will be reluctant to be associated with it. Claims and complaints will be another symptom of poor working relationships. Internally, people will spend time in negative situations rather than building the business and earning fees. Rumours will abound with people whispering to each other at the coffee machines and in the kitchen. As a result, good people will not feel in tune with the values of the organisation and, seeing no future worth having, will leave. Absenteeism will increase as the impact of working in such a negative atmosphere affects people's health and stress levels.

One firm I was asked to help had found itself at an employment tribunal three times within one year. It seemed too much of a coincidence that they were having such a problem so often. One cause could have been poor employee recruitment processes. However, I discovered that the actual cause was sexist behaviour by one of the partners. Their Management Board felt the solution lay in assertiveness training for the staff rather than tackling the partner in question. I advised that I was not willing to do this as, unless we could address the bad behaviour, I would not succeed in eradicating the problem. They agreed to let me meet with the individual concerned. The partner told me that he was simply overwhelmed with work and thought that his behaviour had been taken *'out of context'*. When the impact was pointed out to him, he accepted that he needed help with his workload and agreed to stop this unacceptable way of behaving.

I do not want to create the picture from the above example that only men are the cause of bad behaviour. Women are equally guilty of this, especially verbal harassment and victimisation. One female partner was so arrogant that she tapped her coffee cup in a client meeting to indicate to her trainee that she wanted more coffee. The client who gave me this example said he was so embarrassed by the incident that, when the partner left the room, *he* felt he had to apologise for *her* behaviour. This resulted in the trainee feeling even more awkward.

Addressing bad behaviour is a difficult but essential task. It will require tackling strong-minded individuals about what might well be a very personal issue. As a result, this will inevitably require our leaders and managers to have the ability to deal with conflict.

4.6 Managing conflict constructively

People working together will always lead to some conflict, especially where the work is demanding, difficult and time-pressured. Many professionals have become comfortable with conflict, seeing it as an inescapable part of our working lives and as a result, inured to its effect on other people. It is therefore important to deal with the conflict on open terms and in a planned way. As a result, good managers and leaders must have the ability to manage conflict and manage it constructively.

Dealing with conflict is never easy. Even those of us who appear to enjoy a good argument can feel drained at the end of a day of endless hassle and debate. Too many people have become resigned to stress as a necessary part of their working lives. Stress is one of the underlying causes of the bad behaviour we have considered above. The test of any manager or leader is the way that he or she tackles competing priorities and conflict. Most firms will have at some point to deal with underlying tensions. Some partners may feel that others are not pulling their weight, others that the firm needs to generate more profits and others that life is becoming too unpleasant. Unfortunately these issues will not go away, but will fester and surface often at the wrong moment for a seemingly irrelevant reason.

Most people and organisations work better under positive pressure, as we need to stretch ourselves and be stretched to produce our best work. Healthy debate is necessary for us to run successful firms as people should feel committed to what they do and where they want to be in the future. As a result, they should want to be part of the decision-making process. We *need* their energy and commitment, as we do not want to employ robots that simply turn up and do what they are told. Just as too much conflict is exhausting, the absence of conflict is also a cause for concern.

Most of us, however, have to cope with too much, rather than not enough, conflict. Professionals are trained to analyse and debate issues, to stand their ground to protect the interests of their clients and their profession. As a result, many have a habit of arguing for arguing's sake. They have a tendency to intellectualise problems, not seeing the 'bigger picture' or the impact of their apparent disagreement. Many of us will identify with meetings where one person takes up time and distracts other people's energy by making esoteric points, which contribute nothing constructive.

Professional partnerships are like marriages. People spend a great deal of time in each other's company, often under demanding time and client constraints. As a result, people need to understand each other, what they are trying to achieve and be prepared to recognise each other's strengths and support any weaknesses. When the firm has too much work, tension and conflicting priorities are inevitable. Similarly, when profits are under pressure, some people will feel that they are carrying other partners, which can also result in conflict and unhappiness. Like successful marriages, people must be prepared to support each other through good and bad times. Like most relationships, trigger points can appear to be trivial with tempers flaring out of proportion to the alleged problem. For example, the need for and timing of internal meetings can cause considerable tensions when people already feel under pressure. As a result, people attend with a less than positive attitude towards the topic under discussion. It is essential therefore to establish as stress free a working environment as possible and be sympathetic to peoples' workloads when scheduling any routine meetings.

4.6.1 Identify the sources of conflict

It is important to work out the sources of any conflict. These will include both resource and people issues. For example, computer failures can cause considerable tensions amongst working relationships, triggering bad temper and frustration. It is important to identify the real source, not just the apparent source that makes the most noise. Sometimes apathetic behaviour will be an underlying cause of tension, which manifests in considerable noise from other people and departments. In most organisations, people are all too aware of the 'hot spots' with the result that they receive all the attention. However, the apathetic or 'cold spots' also need to be sorted out as they may be causing some of the frustrations which are triggering the hot spots! We need to draw a visual Conflict Map of interconnected relationships and triggers. These may well include:

- inter-departmental client communications,
- current operational workloads,
- IT back up, accessibility to data, filing, speed of processing,
- month and year-end targets and invoices,
- weekly computer back ups and printouts,
- access to print room equipment,
- timing of annual appraisals or review processes, and/or
- holiday or illness cover.

This mapping exercise will begin to show up the underlying causes, as for example, there may be a scheduling problem that is creating a bottleneck of demand, such as Friday afternoons or month ends. There may well be a small number of key individuals who appear in many of the 'hot spots'. There may also be a group of people who specialise in negativity and not doing key tasks they have been allocated.

(a)   Fight versus flight

As we all know, people tend to respond to stressful situations in the same way that our ancestors did – in other words, we fight the enemy or run away very fast. Those of us who prefer to fight are seen as the main causes of conflict. Yet, those of us who run away have as much responsibility. I know from experience how irritating it can be to work with people who avoid confronting a genuine problem. What tends to happen is that the more they run away, the more annoyed I become. What 'fighters' have to appreciate is that 'flight' people are genuinely scared of conflict and 'flighters' need to understand that running away only makes the situation worse.

Some people are therefore more comfortable with conflict than others and a result, simply fail to see or appreciate the impact it has on others. They will pursue a point of disagreement beyond any reasonable result, oblivious to the effect on other people and long-term relationships. However, those who prefer to avoid conflict also cause difficulties and resentment. They fail to understand that debate does not mean that there is a fundamental problem or underlying concern about the relationship. Good managers have therefore to be able to identify when argument and debate is healthy, and when it will be extremely damaging to relationships within the organisation. I often hear of examples where people 'win the battle but lose the war'– where a partnership discussion goes completely off the rails and results in fundamental damage being caused to long-term relationships.

(b)   Making mistakes

There are additional tensions associated with professionals and how they handle making mistakes. Risk management will be dealt with more fully in Chapter 5. However, for the purpose of this Chapter, it is important to recognise its impact on conflict and behaviour. Professionals are trained *not* to make mistakes. Given the importance of the services we provide, the impact of making a mistake can be significant – for both the client and the professional involved. As a result, when a mistake occurs this inevitably produces a stress response. This tends to fall into three categories as people respond by:

1.   blaming themselves,
2.   blaming other people, or
3.   hiding their mistakes.

All can result in conflict. The people who blame themselves begin to question their own judgement, and become hesitant and insecure. People who blame other people seek to absolve themselves from responsibility and take nothing to do with solving the problems caused and those few who hide their mistakes generate considerable damage and annoyance when it eventually comes to light.

Good risk management requires all of these issues be tackled, as best practice implies that mistakes are acknowledged and that people (and the organisation) learn from them to prevent a re-occurrence. Those people who blame themselves must learn that we human beings will make mistakes. We do not need to put on 'sackcloth and ashes' and run around berating ourselves as apologising once is usually enough for most people! Those who blame other people must learn to take responsibility for their own actions, and appreciate that when they do this, people will be willing to help them. In my view, those who hide mistakes are the worst offenders. No professional person should run away from admitting a mistake. The test of our professionalism is in the way that we deal with the mistake. Two things are important. The first is to sort out the problem caused by the mistake and the second is to ascertain why it happened and ensure that it will not happen again.

(c)   Underlying causes and tensions

Conflict can also be the result of deeper underlying problems and tensions. We have already considered that what may present as the apparent source of the conflict may mask the underlying cause, which may relate to past history or 'old baggage'. It is important to get at the root of the problem as otherwise energy will be taken up finding a solution to that particular situation, yet the conflict will simply resurface somewhere else. I can think of one difficult partner who appeared to have a problem with one partner in particular. After we resolved the tensions between them, difficulties then presented themselves with her behaviour towards another partner. When I pursued this issue with her, the troublesome individual simply wanted to retire from business but was not open enough to admit it.

4.6.2 Tackle them and allow people to learn

The essential point when faced with underlying tensions within the firm is, as we discussed above, not to avoid dealing with them. The situation will simply worsen with some people copying the extreme behaviour which appears to be tolerated, and others suffering stress-related illnesses and/or leaving the firm, which then adds to stress levels all round. Tackling these tensions requires a co-ordinated effort from a group of key people within the firm who must adopt an objective approach to resolving the problem.

First of all, we must work from an objective and factual basis. We have established that professionals are trained to debate issues. It is essential that where debate is required that we de-personalise it. We should not, for example, wait until one of our female partners is pregnant to try to agree a maternity clause in our partnership agreement, nor wait until the senior partner wants to retire to start talking about succession issues. It is important therefore to deal with specific difficulties in a structured and informed way. As we would with any client problem, we need to prepare fully for any discussion, working from established facts and hard data rather than subjective opinions. Professionals have intellectual abilities, which allow them to think conceptually. These should be harnessed in a positive sense, rather than left to generate esoteric points of debate. The protagonists often do not realise until it is too late the damage that has been done by a subjective and irrational argument.

Quite often, tensions are created through a lack of understanding. For example, some people think they work harder than anyone else. It is important therefore to communicate the facts. For example:

1.   setting targets and publishing actual work-in-progress and fees recovered can illustrate what everyone contributes to achieving targets,
2.   where partners have management responsibilities, the firm should value these,
3.   where people introduce new business, these successes should be made public, and
4.   where people take responsibility for training young professionals and support staff, this should also be recognised.

As much useful information as possible should be communicated to everyone. Again, care has to be taken about how this is achieved. Overloading people with information can in practice create more conflict.

Secondly, to tackle conflict in a co-ordinated way, managers need to sort out the *Process* issues, where scheduling or lack of resources is causing problems from the *People* issues. It is important to start with a few at a time rather than try to do everything at once. As a result, we should prioritise those areas where everyone will see direct benefits quickly.

For example, *Process* issues may require a re-routing of resources or where that is not immediately possible, an acknowledgement that the problem exists. Where resources are constrained, then it important to ask people to come up with constructive solutions rather than allow them to demand that other people (i.e. their managers) come up with answers.

People issues should not necessarily be resolved by adopting a 'sheep dip' approach to tackling behaviour or training issues. We have already identified the importance of setting standards of acceptable behaviour. Aggression, arrogance and rudeness are unlikely to be amongst them, regardless how senior we are in the organisation. Similarly, sending everyone on time management or assertiveness training, even where managers feel that people are working without consideration for other people's time pressures, will cause resentment and potential conflict. It will irritate the 'good guys' who *are* working with consideration for others and will waste a lot of the firm's time and money. It is much more effective to isolate the troublemakers and deal with them directly, either through direct training or one-to-one discussions.

The 'fighters' often require education in self-awareness. They have become too comfortable with extreme behaviour, often taking the view that if people cannot handle conflict they do not have the ability to '*make it*' professionally. As a result, they are no longer aware of or simply do not care about the impact of what they do. The 'flighters' may well need education in self-esteem and assertiveness.

Thirdly, it is important to allow people to learn by making and acknowledging mistakes. As we know, professional work is becoming increasingly complex and regulated. It is essential therefore that people be allowed to learn new techniques and skills. This means that people may make mistakes and in a culture of blame, this is a major cause of conflict. '*Why wasn't I told of this before?*' is a common cry of Client Complaint Partners. All partners must be approachable and open to listening to problems. Staff turnover can also be a major cause of conflict. To reduce this, it is important to retain (and train) key people. Again, improving communications and allowing people to learn supports the development of good people.

Every firm has individuals who cause more problems than they are worth – however senior they are. They often promise clients unrealistic deadlines and then opt out of dealing with the internal tensions that causes. They do not take responsibility for managing clients' expectations and blame others for failing to deliver.

Personal distress will often be one of the underlying causes of bad behaviour, so it is essential to find out the root cause of that stress. For example, is it:

- too much work?
- inadequate support?
- problems over internal relationships?
- feeling undervalued?
- worries about money, health or family situations?

A sympathetic ear can help a great deal in these types of situations. It is essential to develop a constructive relationship with the individual concerned and try to agree a way forward. If he or she is unwilling to respond to offers of help, then, in the final resort, that person may have to be asked to leave the firm as the cost of keeping that individual is too high a price to pay.

4.7   Ability to listen and communicate well

All management writers comment on the importance of good communications within an organisation. Great leaders are said to be excellent communicators, sharing their passion and commitment with other people. Yet, even organisations that are regarded as exemplars of best practice often score poorly on internal communications. Some business writers focus on the need for regular staff surveys, staff meetings, internal newsletters and the like. All of these are perfectly laudable attempts to communicate effectively and consistently, but all will be a waste of time and effort if people do not believe that leaders and managers value them for their contribution.

How to give people information is always a difficult choice. Some people want lots of details, others prefer general concepts. Some people want time to read and reflect, other people want to talk things through. Regardless of the quality of the content, whether I trust the person giving me the information colours my perception and what I *'hear'*. Similarly, if I trust the person, often I do not need the same amount of communication with him or her. Given the amount of information we are deluged with on a daily basis, if we are to communicate effectively, we must concentrate on three things. First of all, we must create trust. Secondly, we must look at the quality (not the quantity) of what we give people and thirdly, we must consider our methods of communicating.

Most people can read more quickly than talk. As a result, the best way to disseminate *routine* information is through written summaries. More sensitive information must be presented to people in a sensitive way. For example, our internal people should always be told in advance of any external publicity. To do otherwise implies that they are not trusted and the effect of that message will cause considerable management issues. Motivational messages are more difficult to achieve through the written word. We can all think of examples of formal aspirational management pronouncements, which leave us less than convinced. As a result, we need to speak directly to people when an important message is to be got across. One valuable technique to develop is the ability to tell stories.

4.7.1 The power of the story

Current management gurus (Cohen & Prusak, 2001; Nicholson, 2000) encourage us to focus on the 'power of the story'. Based on how our ancestors passed cultural history to the following generation, stories have always had a key role on how we communicate. They can also illustrate our values and beliefs (Armstrong, 1992).

In Chapter 6, we will discuss the role of the story in developing long-term relationships with our clients. However, it is also a powerful tool for internal communications as illustrated by how quickly gossip (which is one type of story) races round our organisations. Great leaders are often great storytellers.

As a result, we need to think about the message we want to get across – and then, capture it in a story. By using a carefully chosen metaphor we can encapsulate, for example, what we want to achieve for the business. By putting it in the form of a story, rather than an abstract Business Plan, people will remember it and be able to tell it to other people. Properly chosen, it will also emphasise the values of our organisation. For example, to show our people how we define our commitment to 'high quality leading edge professional services', we tell them a story about when one of our people went beyond the terms of the brief to deliver client excellence. As a result, we can contextualise it for them by showing them what we mean in practice. Developing stories is a skill in itself. We can all think of people who are long winded, boring us with pointless details. We can also think of people who use inappropriate humour that embarrasses the listener. Good stories therefore need to:

- be succinct and to the point,
- be directly relevant to us and our firm,
- illustrate the application of our values in practice,
- use humour appropriately,
- be easy to recollect, and
- allow people to feel comfortable retelling them to other people.

We need to work up some stories and using our story tellers, set them off running around our organisations, talking to people. We then need to listen to what people are saying back. Do they think the stories are credible? Do they believe them? In addition, if we listen to what people are talking about, we will also pick up stories from within our organisations.

4.7.2 Learning to listen

Listening is one of the most important skills in communicating and building relationships. As we will discuss in more detail in Chapter 6, clients describe 'being really listened and responded to' as one of the key elements of exceptional service. Too often professionals talk, rather than listen. Quite often meetings consist of 'parallel' conversations, where one person speaks while the other person tolerates the interruption and then takes up his or her position without any attempt to have a genuine discussion. We have already highlighted the importance of listening to the other person's point of view in the above sections on managing conflict and influencing people. We now need to look at the 'art of listening' in more detail.

Good listeners exhibit a range of verbal skills as well as an ability to pick up on non-verbal clues, such as body language and eye contact. As a result, they:

- listen rather than talk,
- set time aside to listen fully to us and do not allow themselves to take interruptions,
- let us take our time,
- focus all their attention on us, lean forward and look attentive,
- let us finish what we want to say and do not interrupt us,
- do not make assumptions nor jump to conclusions,
- make us feel important,
- show us they are listening by the questions they ask us, and

- remember what we tell them, even if it is weeks later.

One supreme example of these skills I directly experienced was when my daughter started at secondary school. I bumped into her new headmaster a couple of months into her first term. Not only did he remember her name, my name and her younger brother's name, he also remembered the name of the family dog, which was with me at the time. That was impressive and I later found out that he worked very hard to achieve this, spending a lot of time remembering individual pupil's details.

All of this seems obvious, so why do people find it so difficult to do? Many professionals exhibit highly driven behaviour. This means that they are impatient, hate waiting and have a tendency to finish other people's sentences for them. As we can process information faster than people can speak, we have excess processing power in our brains, which allows us to think ahead. This can also make it appear that we are not really listening to what people are saying. Sometimes, however, we are bored as we have heard it all before. We may also be distracted by other things on our mind and we may feel the person is taking too long to make his or her point. External noise, the temperature of the room or the lack of comfort breaks may also distract us. And finally, we simply may not like the person or his or her tone of voice. In these circumstances, we do not listen well.

On the other hand, if we are interested in the subject because it is new, challenging or important to us, if we find the person 'personable' and when we are able to listen without distractions, we are able to be attentive and active listeners. To be effective leaders and managers, we need to pay more attention to our active listening skills. First of all, we need to complete a quick self-audit. How well do we really listen? Which of the above bad habits or situations do we need to correct?

4.8   Solve problems and achieve solutions

We now move on to the final management abilities – the ability to solve problems and find acceptable solutions. This leads on naturally from the skills we have already discussed. We have already looked at the importance of gathering accurate information, rather than relying on peoples' subjective opinion. We have also considered the importance of listening to people and what they have to say. Identifying options is an excellent way of involving people in sharing their opinions in a way that forces them to come up with constructive solutions and agree on workable compromises. As a result, we need to be able to gather accurate information, listen to people to ascertain their position and point of view, identify options, and negotiate compromises. This process can apply in formal negotiations as well as everyday interactions where we have to work within budgets and resource constraints. We will look at problem-solving in the context of client relationships in Chapter 6, but at this point, we need to look at how we do this internally in more detail.

4.8.1 Plan ahead

As with any management situation, it is important to plan ahead. As always, we need to know what we want to achieve in the short term and equally important, in the longer term. For example, we may have sufficient resources at the moment, but they may be working ineffectively. We may anticipate an alteration in demand in the future which will require a change in scheduling or work practices. We need to know who will be affected by these changes as well as who will stand in the way of their implementation. Planning ahead allows us to be clear about what we want and prevents us from getting distracted into side issues or problems. To achieve a successful solution requires us to gain commitment from other people and be clear about how we will measure that success.

It is important at the outset to identify as wide a range of options as possible. Knowing the key influencers within our organisations, having their respect and appreciation of our position will help us considerably in generating options. As a result, it is essential to talk to everyone who will be directly or indirectly affected. Even when we are quite clear about what we want, to allow us to build a long-term relationship, we need to know what other people want out of the current and any future situation. Good problem solvers are great listeners. They spend time listening to what people want and reflecting on how that can be achieved. They also need to be persuasive in their arguments, knowing how to present to their audience in a way that illustrates appreciation of their views.

It is also important to think through some 'worse case' scenarios. That is not to say that we have to be negative about the situation, but that to ensure a positive outcome for everyone we need to consider possible future problems. For example, what if our demands change? What if we run into technical problems? We need to have thought through and built in some contingency options. This also helps people realise that whilst, they may not be in complete agreement about what is being proposed, there are other potential solutions which may be less palatable.

4.8.2 Achieve a win – win solution

It is therefore important to achieve a solution that is both practical and workable. Asking the right questions and listening to people allows us to identify possible options and check out how people make decisions. They are also important to allow us to find out what people actually want, rather than what they appear to want. These questioning skills are the same as we use in working with our clients. Professionals are trained to focus in on particular client problems and tend to do so by asking questions which narrow the discussion rather than widen it. However, there are often situations where people may talk about one problem while hiding another underlying issue. To address this, we learn to listen attentively and not make assumptions. Not only does asking questions help us to understand what people want, it also allows us to begin to see it from their perspective. Developing a wide range of options means that everyone can be seen to benefit from the eventual outcomes. It also provides a forum to debate issues, for people to learn to appreciate everyone's position and develop a shared solution. At the end of the day, this will help with subsequent implementation. Agreeing common ground is equally important so that everyone can see the benefits of working together. We must devise solutions that *will* be put into practice.

Compromise on both sides may indeed be required as we work through to the solution. At the end of the day, our working lives and our organisations can never be perfect. As a result, we need to be flexible in our relationships and our dealings. It is important therefore to build in continuing commitment as it may be necessary to go back to what was agreed and amend it because of changing circumstances outwith anyone's control.

In my experience, many managers give of their time and commitment without getting much in return. They often spend many months seeking workable solutions and persuading people to put them into practice. They may be receiving limited thanks and praise for the effort they are putting into effecting key changes. It often requires outsiders to comment positively about how much they have achieved. It is essential that managers also feel that their effort and contribution have been valued. Promoting such successes also helps to reinforce the practical benefits and value of effective leadership and management.

4.9   How to develop these abilities?

We have looked at the six attributes of effective leaders and managers in some detail. Not all will come naturally to all professionals, yet as we move through our professional lives, we are expected to become managers and coaches for younger people and support staff, and most likely, effective leaders in our organisations. As a result, it is important to look at building these skills as we work through each stage of our careers.

In my experience, it is much easier to persuade professionals to improve these skills in the context of developing their client work, rather than label them as 'management skills'. As a result, we should emphasise that all six will be required to succeed with our client-related work and should be built into all of our skills training and career profiles. If we carefully assess our own abilities, reinforce those where we are strong and work at improving those where we are weak, we will become effective managers and leaders of our organisations.

Conclusions

Sustaining effective leadership and management is the key to successful implementation of change. This requires a long-term commitment to building relationships through inspiring trust, managing bad behaviour and conflict, listening and solving problems.

We need to be able to influence people, rather than direct them. We need to reward good behaviour and tell stories that reflect our values and our success. We need to be able to identify solutions that are practical and achievable.

Key Action Points

1.   continually develop our leadership and management skills
2.   always build trust and long-term relationships
3.   identify and work with key influencers
4.   define acceptable behaviour and reinforce it
5.   accept that some conflict is healthy and manage it
6.   allow people to learn
7.   develop listening and story-telling skills
8.   solve problems proactively

5

MAXIMISING OUR RESOURCES

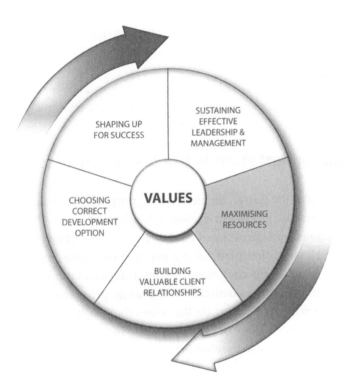

5.1   Introduction

This segment of the Model is important for professional firms because their resources cause them unique management issues. First of all, as most professional firms continue to trade as partnerships, this causes resource limitations and restrictions on the rate and pace of growth where partners have to self-finance expansion plans. Secondly, professionals are trained to be risk averse when advising clients. As a result, what often appears to outsiders to be a viable business risk is voted out by partners who are not comfortable with that choice. And thirdly, partners have a natural interest in agreeing and monitoring how resources are managed and their money is spent.

In Chapter 2, I suggested that firms complete a Resource Audit to identify how well resources are being used. In my experience, common areas of resource wastage include our use of time and people. In this Chapter, I will therefore address these two resources in more detail. I will also look at risk management as any failure to address risks results in resources being hijacked. More fundamentally, resources are often wasted through failure to implement change after time and energy has been invested in agreeing priorities and plans.

We will therefore start this Chapter by looking at how to overcome resistance to change and achieve implementation of plans and action points.

5.2   Implementation is the key to success

As I mentioned at the outset, the underlying purpose of this book is to enable professional firms to implement decisions. Implementation is therefore the key to success. Professional firms need not have simply the ability to plan, but the ability to implement that plan. In my experience, many professionals have developed a cynical approach towards the implementation of change. They have seen management consultants and change programmes come and go, without any perceivable impact on the issues they were supposed to address. With each failed programme or initiative, the cynicism and resistance grows. It is essential for us to be able to rebut this view and prove that positive change is achievable.

In theory, implementing an Action Plan should be easy after the effort put into discussing and agreeing it. Yet most firms find it very difficult to put planning into action. Implementation is difficult in professional partnerships for three reasons. Firstly, the independent nature of professionals implies that we are trained to use our intellect to debate issues. Secondly, the nature of partnerships requires the consensus of the main players and influencers. And finally, most people are resistant to change.

How do we overcome this resistance to change? In theory, we could go out and recruit people who are 'comfortable' with change and not inclined to argue with us. Few of us, however, have the luxury of starting with no existing colleagues. We need therefore, to be able to work in the short term at least, with our existing resources. In most professional firms, people react very badly to being told that they have to change and as a result, need to be *persuaded* to implement decisions.

The high street banks looked at this problem some years ago. Their employees were being asked to cope with a great deal of change, not only in their use of technology but also in their everyday dealings with customers. To help them to become comfortable with change and learning, employees were encouraged to learn anything, for example, another language or cookery, to encourage them to appreciate that regardless of age or experience, it was still possible to acquire new skills. We require to adopt the same approach towards our professional colleagues. It would be foolish of us to rush into their rooms and announce that we are now all going to work in a completely different way. Instead we need to gradually build people's trust and show them the direct benefits of implementing change. Easily said, but how do we actually do it?

5.2.1 The key elements of implementation

Achieving successful implementation works from the premise that we have agreed a long-term focus for the firm and its future success. The best way to achieve that is for the firm to have a robust Business Plan agreed by everyone (see suggested template at the end of Chapter 2). At a minimum, we need to develop a written statement of our long-term goals supported by short and medium-term actions. Spending time on this project will be time well spent, as it will *save* time and resources later by allowing us to have a clear sense of focus.

To implement our plan, we need to:

1. assess priorities, agree sensible timescales and allocate resources,
2. pick particular individuals who have the drive, energy, and skills to achieve them,
3. be careful not to over commit key people or resources,
4. regularly review progress, and offer ongoing and additional support,
5. tell everyone what progress is being made, and
6. once completion has been achieved, publish and celebrate our successes.

Time is finite and cannot be stretched, added to or in some magical way altered. Despite that obvious fact, I constantly see firms attempting to tackle major projects all at the same time and involving the same people. Another major resource problem is energy and enthusiasm. The 'willing horses' can become tired and deflated very quickly if they are surrounded by people who undermine them.

It is essential therefore to prioritise a few key actions, which either directly benefit a large part of the firm and/or address an area of frustration for most people. We need to tackle a few at a time, targeting those that can be achieved within a short time scale of say, three months. It is important to let people see *that things actually happen*, not merely get talked about happening. As a result, whatever action is chosen must be capable of being achieved in a demonstrable way. For example, *'improving staff communications'* is a stated target in most operational action plans, but how will we know that that particular project has worked? Because people talk more … or less? Because people spend more…. or less time round the coffee machines? Because more or less internal emails are sent? Therefore, to demonstrate and track its effect we must at the outset, establish how we will measure its effect. For example, to track improvements in communications we could:

- set up a small focus group and check in with them regularly,
- ask people at their annual appraisals if they perceive any change,
- monitor the amount of internal emails, and/or
- ask people to give examples of any improvement.

Once people see that change can be implemented and they directly benefit from it, they are much more likely to believe in and help with the next set of actions. It is essential therefore that these first initiatives do not drift or fail. People must not be allowed to revisit the original decision, nor get distracted discussing other options. It is important for leaders and managers to be patient and at the same time determined – a combination of charming the dissenters and encouraging the procrastinators. It is our job to keep the momentum going, sorting out any internal resource conflicts and ensuring that the 'willing horses' are properly supported *and* recognised for their efforts. If the project is important, it should be afforded that priority.

On completion, all benefits and successes should be promoted and talked about. People who have contributed should be rewarded and any internal targets should recognise and value the time dedicated to this undertaking. As a result, it will be possible to move on to the next priority actions, allocating these to a wider group of people so that more and more of the firm becomes comfortable with change and the successes it brings. Accordingly, it is essential to tackle projects that have a high 'win' factor for everyone.

The rest of this Chapter is dedicated to looking at projects that release resources. Given the current pressures on time and energy, I would suggest that we start by identifying and implementing projects that *result in* saving people's time.

5.3   Time Audit

Time is quite literally money for any professional service firm. As with any service organisation, the most precious resource is people's time. Time is finite and however hard we all work we cannot manufacture more time in a working day, week, month or year. We can however, make sure that time is not wasted, by ensuring that:

- basic systems and procedures are in place to allow people to be clear about what they should and should not do,
- up to date, useful, accurate and accessible styles and templates have been developed which people know how to access and use, and
- people have the technology and skills needed to work effectively.

However, in my experience, in a typical working week, a busy professional will spend at least two hours a day on non-productive work. At any hourly rate, this annualises to a great of money. Even if all of it cannot be directed into fee-earning work, much of it can be better spent – in reading, learning, and/or developing new clients and contacts. Time wasters include cumbersome and inefficient systems and procedures, poor work habits of the firm or certain individuals and ineffective use of existing resources. In addition, professionals 'waste' time undertaking tasks that their clients regard as adding little or no value to their service delivery. Finally, it is important to ensure that people spend their time on work they enjoy because we can do what we enjoy faster and with much less effort than what we dislike doing.

Therefore, the first area to tackle is everyone's use of time. Achieving better use of time has two advantages – firstly, it means that people become more productive and secondly, it allows them the time, the energy as well as the inclination to tackle other operational (and strategic) projects.

Any change in work practice cannot produce more actual hours in the week. However, if we review and adjust how time is being spent, the benefits to us and our firms are significant. These include:

1.   increased response times and quality of work,
2.   increased profitability of client work and fee recovery,
3.   increased client satisfaction, service levels and referrals,
4.   increased job satisfaction, sharing of information and morale,
5.   decreased write off of work-in-progress and non-recoverable time,
6.   reduction in client complaints and claims,
7.   reduction in hours worked in the office (and at home), and
8.   energy and time released to do other things.

All of this will benefit our relationships with other people, both directly through a feeling of satisfaction of work well done and indirectly through a reduction in overall stress levels. Time is a finite commodity and should not be wasted. It is essential for any firm to constantly review its use of time. Longer hours in the office are not the answer to underperformance or poor profitability. Poor systems and procedures should be adjusted to support rather than frustrate people. Bad work habits should be challenged and exemplars of effective use of time developed. Clients should be asked to define what they see as time well spent. Overall our ultimate aim should be to get to the end of a normal working week with a feeling of time well spent.

It is important to claw back time for everyone. This will release energy and generate commitment for tackling more. The opposite effect will be achieved if everyone is exhausted and frustrated. In my experience, long hours in the office continue to be the norm in many professional offices. Research into risk management and stress highlight that tired (and stressed) people make mistakes. Certainly trying to complete work when we are tired takes a lot longer. We can all recollect a situation when we stayed late to do something which when we read it through the following morning was not our best work.

Let us start with working through the process of the Time Audit as it is essential to analyse our use of time, both internally and externally, identify bottlenecks and time stealers and tackle them.

5.3.1 Analysis

We must start by speaking to people to find out where they think time is being lost and/or hijacked. If asked, most people (especially support staff) can easily identify where time is being lost every day, every week and every month.

We can also use our existing reporting systems to help us. Most firms now have some method of recording time. Properly computerised, this provides a huge amount of useful information about:

- where people are spending too much time,
- where some types or stages of work are taking too long,
- where work is being duplicated or corrected,
- where time is being wasted on work that is not valuable to us,
- where time is being wasted on work that is not valuable to our clients, and
- where time is being lost because of poor administration and/or systems.

It is essential to be able to evaluate where time is being lost and more importantly, how this can be stopped. For example, the introduction of technology was supposed to save us time – and in many cases, it has. Whilst most fee earners now have direct access to a PC to allow them to deal with their own emails and letters, some have not been given sufficient training. A few years ago very little of our time was taken up dealing with emails, yet now most of us regularly stay late or work at home after hours catching up on their backlog.

First of all we need to look at how we are spending our time. Firms who use computerised time recording have a time advantage here as most computerised systems are sophisticated enough to give us much of this information in routine reports. Individual and departmental printouts can identify specific areas of difficulty and allow us to seek the answers to a number of questions. The answers will indicate where changes need to be made.

Where chargeable targets are not being met:

- Is it because people do not have enough client work to do?
- Are workloads spread unevenly?
- Are people finding delegation difficult?
- Why is so much time taken up on 'non-chargeable' work?
- Do people understand how to operate any formal system?
- Do they have enough time (!) to record time properly?
- Were the targets realistic?

Where chargeable targets are being met or exceeded:

- Is the firm able to fully recover those hours?
- If not, why are clients not being asked to pay the full fee?
- Do clients pay without question and on time?
- Do clients come back to us for repeat work?
- If exceeded, are people spending too long on client work?
- Are they being asked to do work they do not know how to do?
- Are they spending time 'reinventing the wheel' because styles and templates are difficult to access?
- Are the systems slow and cumbersome to use?
- Are fee earners typing their own work because of delays in central typing?

Secondly, an overview of everyone's timesheets will illustrate where people and departments are working effectively and where there are problems. Some people simply seem to be better at organising their workloads, at getting files processed, at charging and recovering a fair fee. It is important to identify why this is the case. For example, that person or department may be good at delegating work to the correct level, training staff and keeping clients advised about costs and timescales. What works for them can be distilled and applied across the rest of the firm. Whilst I accept that it is easier to 'process' more simple client work, such as debt recovery or audit work, it is equally important to manage some of the risk of complicated and sophisticated work by putting in place good checklists and training.

Systems and work practices also need to be looked at to see where time is being lost and/or where people feel frustrated about wasting time. If people are becoming irritated by slow computer software, the constant interruption of internal emails or background noise in open plan offices, then these distractions need to be resolved. Inevitably time will be lost when people feel they cannot concentrate on difficult work, struggle to get through routine paperwork or spend time away from their desks moaning to other people about these problems. Internal systems should support staff not exhaust them!

In addition, we need to ask clients where they see value for money. We have covered this point in general terms in Chapter 2 and will deal with it in more detail in Chapter 6. Professionals continue to be reluctant to ask clients for this sort of information, yet those firms who do speak directly to clients comment on how useful the exercise is and how much they learn as a result. Face-to-face interviews with key clients allow us to ask open questions about what aspects of our service they value and which seem of limited use. This information must be fed back into our service delivery to allow us to re-allocate where we spend our time. The findings will offer considerable help with reducing the amount of time wasted on tasks that clients see of no value, particularly in relation to the generation and content of paperwork.

5.3.2 Identification of bottlenecks and time stealers

Completing our Conflict Map (see Chapter 4) will have highlighted a number of areas where bottlenecks occur and/or where time is wasted because of resource problems, such as printing availability. Schedules and workflows for areas where a number of people have competing demands for resources should be developed and promulgated. The Finance Department, in particular, will experience significant month-end pressures, some of which can be avoided if people think ahead and consider other people's workloads.

In many cases, it is the professionals themselves who cause problems. Most support staff know how long it takes to complete a routine task, such as putting a proposal together, yet fee earners seem not to (or choose not to) remember. During a training session on time-management, one partner's secretary flagged up she was frustrated having to rework client proposals again and again. She knew that it took a minimum of four hours to turn the amendments around, yet her partner regularly came to her with it at 5.00pm. She had tried to tell him this without success and felt that he was being demanding and selfish. Her colleagues suggested that she should put up a sign saying "4 HOURS!" above her desk, which she did, allowing humour to help to defuse the situation.

Similarly, partners and senior managers may be causing bottlenecks by doing too many routine tasks themselves. As a result, it is essential to look at signing authorities for formal letters and client reports, for example, so that fee earners do not become frustrated when after all their efforts the letter or report does not go out to the client who is expecting it.

5.3.3 Tackle them

Once these issues have been identified, the firm needs to make changes. Systems may need to be adjusted, IT training given, delegation improved, bad habits and behaviours addressed. In many cases, people simply have got used to poor working practices. This does not necessarily mean that the firm has an aggressive work culture. Some 'happy and helpful' firms are very inefficient with people rushing in and out of each other's rooms to talk through the last telephone call or email. Everyone spends their day trying to help each other with the result that little is achieved.

In other cases, however, selfish behaviour has been tolerated without comment. Certain individuals steal time from other people, often by hijacking their staff resources or dumping their poor time management on other people to sort out. Managing partners complain to me of their own time being *'leached away'* persuading people to do what they should be doing as a matter of course. Tackling poor performance continues to be a major part of most managers' daily workload.

Monitoring workloads is essential. In general terms people work better when they have 110% of what they can easily cope with. More than that causes high levels of stress. Less than that, professionals become bored and disruptive. If people are working long hours and still being unproductive, the whole culture and work practice of the firm has to be investigated and adjusted.

Let us look in more detail at the two areas people always mention as time (and energy) wasters – emails and meetings. For most organisations, tackling them would benefit our organisations and make us extremely popular with everyone!

(a)   Emails
Emails are becoming a serious highjacker of time with most people describing them as one of the most disruptive, annoying and tiring aspects of their day.

They come in at all hours of the day and night, many are of limited relevance and interest with the result that it is difficult to prioritise them. Time is even taken up deleting them!

As a result, we must develop a plan to tackle our use of emails, identify where they are wasting time and where they add value and save time. It is important to identify ways of managing them, through general screening systems or 'batching' them. Client emails have to be given priority, internal emails less so. If at all possible, the timing of internal emails should be considered and regulated. Most routine internal emails could be batched and sent out at the end of the working day rather than constantly interrupting people. (Intranets try to achieve the same end result). This would allow people to concentrate on client work during the day. Again, providing IT training helps people operate their software so that for example, internal messages immediately get sorted into a 'read later' folder.

(b)   Meetings

For most of us, meetings take up an inordinate amount of our working days, yet many of us experience little progress or sense of achievement as a result of attending them. The problems with meetings lie partly in the processes we adopt and partly in how people affect their dynamics. People get into bad habits when it comes to attending meetings. They become so used to having to endure them that they have no expectation of achieving anything worthwhile. Poor chairing is also a contributing factor. People assume the role of chair without any understanding of what is involved and how to behave. There is nothing more likely to cause a 'bad' meeting than poor chairing.

Meetings are often held without any real purpose. Sometimes, people call them as an excuse to appear to be doing something, and as a result, involve people without any clear idea of who they want to attend and why. Often, no one is entirely sure what was agreed and what the next step will be. We also get into bad habits about following up on the outcomes of meetings. One large professional organisation I know meets every two months with the Minutes of the past meeting being sent out with the agenda for the next one. As a result of this process, it is hardly a surprise that little progress on action points is made.

Too many organisations call meetings without any regard for people's availability or what they want to achieve. Calling a meeting becomes a substitute for doing something – as if the act of calling a meeting is sufficient to show activity! Meetings are often scheduled at inappropriate times. For example, I like to work on my most difficult tasks in the morning. I therefore find attending tedious meetings mid morning particularly frustrating. Other people like to do creative work later in the day and as a result, will be resentful if asked to sit in on a meeting then. It is important to plan meetings with sympathy to people's workloads and personal deadlines, otherwise they will not attend with a positive attitude.

In all cases, we need to check whether holding a meeting is the best way to deal with the problem. In some instances, the meeting has become more important than the problem and may well be preventing proper discussion. Any meeting, which is not serving a real purpose, must be discarded.

The process used must also support good use of time with paperwork sent out ahead of the formal meeting, the right level of people attending and clear action points and follow up agreed. In my experience, using flipcharts to record what is being discussed reduces the time spent in meetings by thirty percent.

To tackle meetings, we therefore need to carry out a formal Meeting Audit. To undertake this, we need to:

1.   find out how many routine meetings there are, how long they take and who they involve,
2.   sort them into two categories – those we need to have and those we do not,
3.   discontinue those we do not need,
4.   check that those we do need involve the correct people and take place at acceptable times,
5.   ensure that papers are sent out in good time, and that suitable rooms and flipcharts are available, and
6.   resolve that all meetings will take no longer than two hours and that written Action Points are issued within one working day.

Meetings used constructively allow people to share expertise, learn from each other, and produce creative and practical solutions to problems and issues. When meetings perform less well, they cause bad feeling, frustration and unpleasantness that extend beyond the actual meeting itself.

5.4   Focus on achieving results

Another way to maximise our use of resources stems from the feedback we receive from our Client Service Audits. As a result, clients will have told us what they value and where they want us to spend our time. They will have emphasised the need to achieve results, and of using our skills and knowledge to devise innovative solutions. We need therefore to use internal processes to help us delegate and free up our time to work on areas where we can add value to our client services.

It is therefore important to focus on changing the way that we work and the work that we do. Prior to the introduction of accessible technology, many professionals had to spend time carrying out routine calculations or completing draft documents and drawings. The working day of all of the professions has changed. For example, accountants do not have to manually produce financial spreadsheets and accounts, lawyers do not need to spend time comparing earlier drafts against later versions, and architects do not have to redraw detailed drawings to reflect one small change in design. As a result, we need to look at what we, and more particularly, our clients want us to achieve. For example, the whole emphasis of time for many accountants has shifted from the production of financial information to its interpretation, and for architects from the production of drawings to the generation of design.

I accept that we cannot simply focus on what our clients ask us to do. We need to be able to balance that with professional risk management. Complying with the rules and regulations of our professional bodies is equally important. We need therefore to develop systems and styles that allow us to cover our backs while *at the same time* focus on achieving a successful outcome for our clients. Using templates and checklists, working to external quality standards and/or joining associations which share best practice can all help. Most importantly however, some one within the firm needs to maintain an overview of what work is done, when and how. Key questions which need to be asked include:

1.   do we need to continue to do this task?
2.   if yes, what is the most appropriate way to do it?
3.   once that is decided, who is the most appropriate person to do it?
4.   does that person need any additional support and/or training?
5.   how will we ensure that the work is properly supervised and checked?

This is where delegation can pay great dividends. The ability to delegate effectively is an essential skill for any professional. In my experience, too often delegation becomes abdication with senior professionals asking more junior people to undertake tasks without adequate support or supervision. This is therefore an important area for any training programme and/or career development.

5.5   Speed, accuracy and consistency

Another aspect of our use of time is the need to balance speed with accuracy and consistency. No one will argue with the statement that clients expect us to respond to and process their work faster every year. Those of us who are in our early fifties will remember the introduction of the telex. Before that clients contacted us by letters which were delivered twice a day, and by telephone during normal working hours of 9.00am (sometime 9.30am and shut for lunch!) and 5.30pm at the very latest. Now we have clients phoning us on mobile phones and sending us emails after hours and at weekends – and expecting an immediate reply.

Regardless of whether we think this is a good development or an appalling nightmare, clients judge us on our speed of delivery. As we have discussed before, it is important to educate our clients about how and when they can access us. For example, many firms set out standards of service which specifies how long it will take to return calls, respond to emails, faxes or letters. It is essential therefore for office systems and practices to facilitate our accessibility, not hinder it. I continue to hear stories of Luddite behaviour, for example, senior partners unwilling and unable to use their voice message retrieval system and accidentally erasing two days worth of client messages. I still see professionals using their secretaries to send routine acknowledgement letters by email (which always poses the question in my mind of *'does this allow them to charge more for them?'*). Voice mail can be an excellent way of freeing up the switchboard and preventing clients from hanging on waiting while the person they are phoning is found. However, if we work from the presumption that sometimes a client wants to do more than leave a message (i.e. speak to his or her professional), it must be used in such a way that our clients feel that we are accessible. Voice messages should therefore, be updated on a daily basis to give indications of when individuals are available and when they are not, so that clients do not feel they ware working in a vacuum. When people are on holiday, other people should be able to fully access their emails and voice messages, to avoid any breakdown in communication.

Speed of response has to be balanced with quality and accuracy of response. Protocols have to be developed to deal with incoming and outgoing emails to address risk management issues. Junior professionals must know what they can and cannot do without referral or authorisation. Standards of language must be adopted, erring on the side of being more formal rather than less, as clients are paying us for a professional service after all.

Consistency of response is also important. Clients should see uniformity of approach – by telephone, in writing or at meetings and regardless of who they are dealing with. We will develop the concept of consistency in the context of cross-selling in the next Chapter. Consistency is important to professionals as well as clients. Few of us have the time to start everything we do from scratch. We have already discussed the importance of knowledge management and its current vogue with management gurus. The professions have always been knowledge workers in the sense of sharing knowledge and expertise, either directly by teaching and working with young professionals, or more indirectly through writing and publishing. Therefore it makes sense to create and use templates for routine correspondence, presentations and documents. It also makes sense from the risk management point of view, with the caveat that such templates are used properly and intelligently – not used to abdicate thought, care and attention.

We will now move on to consider Risk Management in more detail as it has a direct effect on how much of our time can be hijacked 'putting out fires'.

5.6   Risk management

Risk management has achieved a higher and more formal profile in recent years. This is partly a response to the increase in claims and complaints resulting in our professional bodies and indemnity insurers asking us to adopt more formal systems. It also results from increased time pressures and complexity of professional work.

Risks stem from a number of inter-related areas. They can result from a failure to manage operational issues such as staff turnover or deliver a quality service.

They can also result from a disregard of legal or regulatory requirements such as compliance with professional body regulations or health and safety issues. It is important therefore to look behind the particular cause of concern and identify the underlying problem. For example, a firm may have recently merged. People on one side of the business may be unhappy about adopting the 'other side's' internal computer systems. As a result, the firm's failsafe diary system will not be adhered to with the potential risk of missing crucial deadlines. No amount of tinkering with or training in the software will alleviate this risk. Only by addressing the underlying agenda of resentment will the risk be managed.

Risk management has become a topic in its own right with firms expected, particularly for insurance purposes, to show how they:

- analyse risk,
- assign ratings to different types of work and/or clients,
- tackle exposed areas,
- prevent their re-occurrence,
- standardise work, and
- train and support people.

Worryingly, only a small number of professional firms admit to having in place formal policies for the management of risk. Even worse, some firms continue to adopt an ostrich like approach to client engagement, taking on work without agreeing a clear brief, costs and timescales. It is important to develop a Risk Management Policy which details how risks are assessed, what criteria are applied, how corrective action will be undertaken and what support is available.

Where risk management has been formalised, in many cases the focus and emphasis is on putting procedures in place rather than tackling the underlying causes of claims and complaints. Procedures will help to prevent risk but people aspects also have to be addressed. As a result, it is essential to educate everyone in the firm about risks and encourage everyone to take responsibility for tackling them.

Risk management is therefore composed of three main aspects:

1. Health and Safety issues including stress,
2. mistakes, and
3. client management.

5.6 1 Managing stress

I do not intend to dwell on physical risks except to remind people that stress now has to be included under the heading of Health and Safety and given as much priority as accidents. Sadly, stress continues to feature in the lives of many professionals, given current workloads, time pressures and increased likelihood of claims and complaints against us. Whilst working under some pressure is important, working under too much pressure continuously damages our physical and mental health, and our relationships with our colleagues and our families. In addition, we have to remember that many of our clients are stressed. Life changes, such as death, divorce and moving house and any type of important money transactions are rated as highly stressful. It is our job to manage that stress, not be surprised by or add to it.

Stress arises where there is a perceived imbalance between the demands being made on us and the resources we have available to us. These include the physical resources as well as our own abilities and skills. Stress impacts on our attention and judgement. Much of what we do is complex and requires the ability to think clearly. Stress increases the risk of making mistakes.

Professionals hate making mistakes. Making a mistake seems to us to imply that we are incompetent and/or careless. Professional indemnity insurance may provide us with some comfort if we make a mistake that results in some form of monetary claim, but it cannot truly protect us from the loss of face or reputation associated with making an error of judgement. As a result, making a mistake affects our confidence in our ability to make judgements, which can lead to further stress. Stress and mistakes are therefore inter-related. Making a mistake:

1. causes us stress, which in turn
2. affects our concentration and memory, which in turn
3. reduces the amount of attention available, which in turn
4. leads to further mistakes.

Mistakes can be acts of omission as much as commission – professionals simply failing to do something they do 99% of the time and/or making assumptions about an individual client or situation. In these cases, putting in place more checklists or failsafe procedures may help, but in many cases, the people who are so overwhelmed that they forgot to do something in the first place are likely to feel even more overwhelmed if they are given detailed procedure manuals to follow! As discussed in Chapter 4, it is important therefore to put in place a culture of support when a mistake is made. People must feel that they can admit to a mistake and get help to deal with it and its consequences.

5.6.2 Dealing with mistakes

Mistakes can be the result of carelessness, thoughtlessness, making assumptions, and/or ignorance. For example, poor delegation can result in the wrong paperwork being sent out or a deadline being missed. People may not be technically competent to do the type of work they are being asked to do or too stressed to think properly. In every organisation, it is essential to manage these risks by doing our best to prevent people being careless, thoughtless, sloppy or ill-informed.

Most of the time, a mistake once made can be easily corrected or sorted out with the client. A simple apology is usually enough, an explanation of what went wrong, an offer to correct it and a waiver of any fee satisfies most clients if dealt with quickly and honestly.

Indeed looking at many of the complaints that end up before professional bodies or PI insurers, many of us would say *'there by the grace of God go many of us!'* Formal complaints often stem from poor client management rather than the damaging effect of the mistake itself. The most important aspect of dealing with mistakes is exactly that – *dealing with them*. To achieve that, we need to know about them in the first place. As a result, as discussed in Chapter 4, we must ensure that we operate a culture where mistakes are 'allowed' i.e. where people feel that they can admit that a mistake has been made and know that the support to remedy is available. This must include formal procedures to deal with a formal complaint and informal discussions where the mistake remains internal. Unfortunately, a lot of professional firms operate either at worst, a 'blame' culture or at best, a *'we never make a mistake'* approach to client service, seeing the client as some kind of Tasmanian Devil making unreasonable and irrational demands. As a result, mistakes are often hidden or blamed on other people or departments.

Human beings are, at the risk of stating the obvious, human. We will therefore during the course of our professional and personal lives make mistakes and errors of judgements. It is essential to educate people that *making* the mistake is not the issue. Instead, what is important is how that individual *handles* it i.e. owns up to it, takes responsibility for and learns from it. As we have discussed before, making a mistake both tests and demonstrates our professionalism, with our colleagues judging us by how we deal with it. If we start to blame other people and/or deny being at fault, we will quickly lose their support and understanding.

Most people recognise that mutual support is essential to cope with the vagaries of professional life and workloads. I can think of a number of occasions in my professional life when a kind colleague has helped me with a problem of my own making. Internally people should always feel that it is more acceptable to admit the mistake and ask for help rather than hide it. Effective risk management requires that mistakes are made known to partners and managers, otherwise corrective action and prevention cannot happen.

When a mistake becomes public, either by way of a claim or a formal complaint, an independent and objective member of the firm should be involved. Internal people should not be assumed to be guilty. Similarly, the complaining client should not be assumed to be in the wrong. If the client has taken the time and trouble to complain, it is because he or she is unhappy about the service provided. Whether there has been a technical mistake or not, the quality of service has failed to meet the standard required. We have already developed in Chapter 2 the concept of quality from the client's point of view. However, from the risk management point of view, it is important to accept that some clients are likely to be more risky than others. Can we therefore develop a way of assessing such risks?

5.6.3 Client management

Client management requires exactly that – management of our clients. As we have considered in earlier Chapters, there is a perception that clients now manage us, expecting us to dance to their tune and at their speed. At a minimum, once we decide to take on a client or a piece of work, we must agree a clear brief including the personnel involved, timescales and costings. In addition, I would like to advocate that we take more care *before* we agree to act for a particular client or sector. In my view, one of the best ways to address risk management is in careful selection of *new* clients.

(a)   Risk Assessment Analysis

Selection has to be carried out *before* we start acting for them. Too often, when we are approached to do a piece of work, we say 'yes' without thinking through whether we in fact should take it on.

It is vital to structure our risk assessment of *new clients* before we agree to act. Some of the areas to be concerned about and the questions to pose are illustrated in Table 5.6.3(a).

When we take on new or additional work from *existing* clients, it is also worthwhile checking out the risks involved. We will be able to quickly answer the questions posed in the above six headings from what we already know about them.

Table 5.6 3(a) Risk Assessment of Clients

	Areas to consider	Possible questions
1	Their previous track record	What is their reputation? What other professionals do they use? Why are they moving firms? How many times have they moved?
2	Their level of experience/expertise	Are they educated enough to give us effective instructions? Are they likely to take a lot of hand-holding? Will they be willing to pay for that?
3	Their financial strength	Can they afford us? Are they too powerful? Are we likely to become too dependent on them?
4	Their type of work	Do we have the expertise? Is it work we are keen to develop? Do we have the technology to work with them the way they want?
5	Its profitability	Is it financially rewarding? Will it develop our expertise? Will it offer training for our young professionals?
6	Our association with them	Will they enhance or undermine our reputation? Will they enhance or undermine our image/brand?

It is also important to look at the risks associated with certain types of client work. Our insurers and professional bodies will be able to tell us what they regard as the high-risk areas. In addition, we need to ask whether *we* are suited to and/or capable of doing this kind of work, based on our past performance and track record. If we made mistakes in the past that exposed us to risks related to a specialist area of work, is it wise to take on a high profile piece of work in that area?

Factors to consider therefore include:

1.   the degree of difficulty of the work,
2.   the timescales involved,
3.   who is doing the work,
4.   the client's expectations and how manageable these are,
5.   the client's potential exposure if the project is not successful,
6.   its interaction with other current workloads,
7.   sector specific statistics, and
8.   the type of work statistics.

We will be able to make an educated assessment of the risk as many of these factors are within our direct control. For example, we know what our workloads are and our experience and expertise in specialist areas. We need to manage our clients' expectations about who is doing their work and within what timescale. We can all think of occasions where our firms have been approached by apparently high-powered clients, taken on what turns out to be difficult and dangerous work and sucked into projects with unrealistic timescales and costs.

(b)   Risk Workload Analysis

Some attempt must be made to weigh the risks against the potential benefits. It is important to do this as objectively as possible given the emotional pressures that clients and other people in our firms may put us under. Like any decision, there will be pluses and minuses and a need to balance risk with reward. There may be the potential for considerable success for both parties. There is also the risk of considerable losses. It is essential that a conscious decision is made based on an understanding of the risk involved. It is important to remember that such a risk assessment is particular to individual firms. For example, a firm that has considerable expertise in a niche sector will not rate that type of work high risk where a more general based practice would. Similarly a firm that has invested heavily in training and technology should be able to manage the risk associated with medium-level work through effective delegation.

Table 5.6.3(b) looks at the risks and rewards involved in varying types of client workload. It helps us with our decision whether to undertake the work in the first place, and highlights that if we do, how we need to manage it. A tick indicates that the work is worth taking on *if* properly managed. For example, high risk work which pays high fees has the potential to be valuable but it needs to be handled very carefully by experienced people.

High risk must always be balanced with high fees. Medium risk offers us the potential to manage it in return for other benefits, such as delegation and/or training. Low risk work offers considerable prospect for good returns.

The Matrix also provides guidelines for priorities in resource management. High risk high fee work requires considerable resource investment and continuous attention. Lower rated work can be managed using normal operational practices and procedures, and offers the opportunity for delegation, skills enhancement and training. The shaded line illustrates the route for career progression, with people starting off with low risk work and with experience, moving through to high.

One of the most fundamental problems with risk management is that people

Table 5.6.3(b) Risk Workload Matrix

	High fees	Medium fees	Low fees
High risk	✔ yes but must be handled carefully by experienced people	Is it worth the risk?	Never!
Medium risk	Yes but will this ever arise?	✔ yes as offers the potential to delegate	Is it worth the risk?
Low risk	Yes but will this ever arise?	✔ yes please as should be easy to manage	? possibly as this may provide opportunity for bulk work

seem to think that someone else is responsible for it. Any Health and Safety Officer knows the difficulty of achieving a 'risk aware' culture. Risk management has to be given a higher profile *throughout* the firm, and no longer seen as the sole responsibility of partners and senior managers. Using a model such as this Matrix helps to achieve this by allowing *everyone* within the firm to contribute to effective risk management and understand their role and place within it. Support staff can appreciate that some areas of work will require priority and additional attention to detail. Junior professional staff can see that although apparently working in a routine and less exciting area, there are areas of exposure to risk that they have a responsibility for. For example, it is their job to follow standard procedures and if they know that some of the basic styles are incorrect, it is their job to bring this to the attention of more senior people.

One last comment remains to be made about risk management. Risk management is an ongoing process. It is not sufficient to put in place procedures and hope these will manage risk. There will be a need to constantly review mistakes, complaints and claims, and take action to prevent their reoccurrence. As our firms are in the process of continuous change, we need to manage the risks associated with that. For example, as we have considered in Chapter 3, clients want us to bring innovation to our service delivery. Innovation implies deviating from established practices, which has risk implications. This must be understood and built in to such developments. It may well be worthwhile appointing an internal 'Risk Checker' – someone whose role is to ask 'what if?' questions?

5.7   Right people in the right jobs

People are our most valuable resource and our most flexible. As a result, in this Chapter where we are identifying ways to maximise our use of resources, we must aim to have the right people in the right jobs. This implies that we are clear about what makes people 'right' for our firm and for the roles we ask them to play.

Putting professionals into job descriptions is never easy. Hammer (1988) talks about the independence of professionals and the importance of allowing them to interpret *how* the job will be done. We considered in Chapter 3 the dichotomy we face of attracting and retaining the best people (i.e. for their independence and professional abilities) and at the same time, managing them. Similarly, risk management requires that we introduce consistency into our work practices, with people clear about what is expected of them. At the same time, we want people to be client focused and tailor our services to suit individual clients.

As a result, it is essential to define the high quality professional services that we want people to deliver and identify how we help them achieve that. We should not assume that our people know what we mean and what we offer them in the way of help. I would suggest that every firm should issue a written statement of the individual aspects of its high quality service. This could include, for example, that *'we deliver on time and within budget, that we are known for the accuracy of our advice and that our people are accessible'*. Similarly, a written statement of support available for its professional staff could include that *'we provide excellent IT support and training, that we have a structured career support and mentoring, and offer stress and bereavement counselling'*

These statements can be internal to the firm or part of external information given to clients and contacts. Whatever is written down must mirror what happens in practice, otherwise people will become cynical and demotivated. I can think of a number of examples of firms pitching for work on the basis of their excellent internal communications and team working, where the reality of working in these firms is that the partners promise impossible deadlines to clients leaving it up to more junior staff to take the blame when these are not met.

When people are working at the right level for their skills and abilities, doing what they enjoy, they are much more likely to 'please' clients. Clients want people to care about the work they do for them. We will develop this client definition of high quality professional service in the next Chapter. If people enjoy what they do, this will be apparent to their colleagues as well. Knowledge will be shared, communications will work well and people will focus on the positive aspects of working together. Working in such a supportive environment, people will be willing to learn and take on more responsibility. As a result, the whole firm will benefit, and able to grow and develop. However, the converse is equally true. When people are underperforming and/or working at the wrong level, the knock-on effect will be considerable.

It is important when dealing with underperformance not to make quick judgements based on incomplete information. As we have discussed already, some professionals use their strength of personality to turn opinions into facts. As a result, it is important to establish the facts by obtaining examples of the individual's underperformance. It is equally important to tackle the issue rather than duck it or hope that the problem will disappear.

5.7.1 Developing good people

One of the ultimate aims of good resource management is to develop good people who will benefit the firm in the long term. It is therefore important to take a long-term view about succession, skill requirements and individual development. Professional firms tend to be guilty of not planning ahead in a structured way with the result that subjectivity creeps into the selection and promotion.

As we have identified already in Chapter 2, to manage our people resources effectively, we need to look at our skills base and match it against our current and future client requirements. This Skills Audit should be done formally using information from appraisals, cvs and direct discussions. It should include technical expertise as well as softer skills, such as time management and presentation skills. This mapping out of skills will show us where we are over-qualified and where we have gaps. It will allow us to plan our training to develop our people resources in line with client demands.

As already discussed, young professionals are much more mobile and inclined to respond to firms who offer them individual development. As a result, we should create some kind of career ladder or 'Career Profile', showing them where they are at present and what potential exists for them in the medium to long term (see Chapter 8). It is also important to show that, even from the beginning of their career, they cannot only concentrate on their technical work but must also be aware of the need to develop skills, such as time management. As a result, we need to show them what they need to do and what support, such as their line manager or training, is available to them. As outlined in Chapter 2, moving upwards through a professional firm requires a range of skills and abilities. These include technical and professional skills, the ability to build long-term relationships with clients and external contacts, and an understanding of business.

Conclusions

Maximising our resources requires considerable skill and time investment. Quality people and tangible resources are a scarce commodity for any organisation and require continuous investment and fine-tuning.

Implementing any project which saves time will pay direct benefits in people attitude toward effective management. Focusing on outcomes rather than processes, and ensuring services are delivered with speed and consistency are key priorities for all professional organisations. Risk management includes managing stress and mistakes, coupled with careful client and work type selection. Having the right people in the right job ensures that our people resources are being used to their maximum potential as well as providing the basis of future service delivery success.

Key Action Points

1. any project undertaken must be implemented
2. prioritise projects which release time
3. encourage people not to get into bad habits
4. focus on changing how we process work
5. ensure that we deliver quality as well as speed of response
6. actively manage the risk relating to client work
7. accept that people will make mistakes
8. ensure that we develop our skill base for the future

6

BUILDING VALUABLE CLIENT RELATIONSHIPS

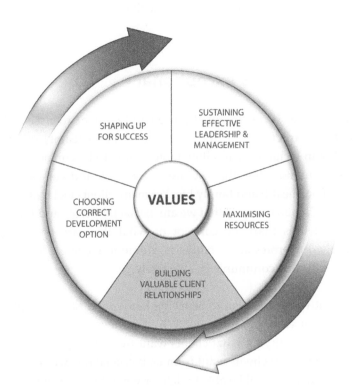

6.1   Introduction

In Chapter 2, we considered the importance of asking our clients what they want from us, and working with them to agree their expectations and establish their trust. In this Chapter, we will look in these issues in more detail with the ultimate objective of allowing us to build valuable relationships with our clients.

All professionals identify strongly with working with clients where there is mutual trust and respect. However, clients now expect us to tailor our services to suit them and most want to know up front how much these services will cost them. We have to respond to that and at the same time, deliver a relationship that produces 'value' for both sides. We need to adapt our traditional ways of working and timescales to match what our clients want and are prepared to pay for. Technology offers one route to achieve this, allowing us to access and manage information in differing ways. However, we have to be wary of using too much technology and losing the personal touch. We will look at this in the context of implementing cross selling to existing clients and how we attract new clients.

6.2   Good versus exceptional

Most professional firms accept the need to be client focussed. Some have adapted their structures to develop client service teams, others invested considerably in technology to allow their people to be contactable 24 hours a day. Most of us now feel that we are at the beck and call of clients to the detriment of our health and family life. Yet many clients feel that we are remote and distant. Clients comment that we are '*not on their side*', and more interested in abstract details than the concept of what they are trying to achieve. Significantly our professional bodies continue to receive a lot of complaints based on a failure to communicate effectively.

Why is it that while we seem to be trying harder and harder to please clients, they still do not value what we do? Why are they so difficult to please? The answer lies in identifying what clients want from their professional advisors. Finding out what our clients want from us is crucial for two reasons. Firstly of all, it ensures that we will be able to deliver what they expect us to achieve for them. Secondly, the quality of our service is dependent on what the client perceives as good value.

In Chapter 2, we defined the three basic steps to developing long-term relationships with our clients, which were to:

1.   establish and agree client's expectations,
2.   develop and retain trust, and
3.   be responsive to their needs.

To compete in today's consumer-orientated market, at a minimum, we need to consistently deliver a high quality professional service. *All* good quality professional service firms should be able to address these three basic steps, through taking initial instructions and developing effective work practices. However, to differentiate ourselves from our competitors, we need to do more than that. We need to think about the last time we used another professional service, and ask ourselves a series of questions:

- Did the professionals involved get to know us as an individual?
- Did they spend time listening to what we had to say – and then, offer a solution tailored to what we had told them?
- Did they take the time to involve us in agreeing what course of action should be taken?
- Were they always available and pleased to respond to us?
- Did they avoid confusing jargon?
- Did they pre-empt some of our concerns and needs?
- Did they think ahead and flag up issues that we should be aware of?
- Did they suggest some practical solutions to current and potential problems?
- Did they show that they cared about our problem?

We need to check these questions against our own service delivery. What clients truly want is for their professionals to be proactive, in other words, to think beyond the matter in hand, focusing on achieving end results rather than the details of the process of getting there. For most firms, these are the clients we want to develop long-term relationships with – the ones who remain loyal to us, use our and their time effectively and refer more business to us. In that way, we will build and maintain their loyalty to us and as a result, build long-term relationships which bring value to *both* parties.

As a result, we need to deliver a service that our clients feel is exceptional. The distinction between good and exceptional is hard to define, as it depends on what each individual client values. For example, one of the aspects that I value if I stay in a '5 star' city centre hotel is that their staff park my car for me, as this saves me time, energy and anxiety. For other people, that '5 star' value may be reflected in the availability of a gym or free access to the Internet. However, there are a number of core elements that all clients agree on.

In my experience, it is worth asking key clients how they define *'exceptional'* as the examples they choose tells us a lot about their individual preferences. For example, I asked one of my senior director clients (an engineer by profession) to describe what he wanted from his professional advisors. He said:

'This is kind of asking the difference between 'that's my right and expectation as a client' i.e. good professional service and the WOW factor where you are really taken by surprise because it's well beyond what you expected.
Criteria
- *very caring client service from the start and then throughout*
- *high quality timely communications*
- *delivered on time*
- *professional reporting, clear, concise, good descriptive English*
- *priced competitively and up front*
- *careful recommendations (beyond the fear of litigation stuff)*
- *precisely agreed contract and carefully specified*
- *relevant support and back up when needed*
- *available when needed or at least user-friendly contactable.'*

As a result, I now know that if I deliver all of these criteria, I will provide him with what he sees as exceptional service. Indeed, he had defined his 'standards of service' for me.

Many of us will look at that list and say that, in essence, what he describes is nothing hard or difficult, yet he finished by saying that *'to be 'wowed' would be a rare occurrence for me and many others!'* It is interesting that he uses the phrase *'caring'*. This is the essence of our relationships with our clients. They want us to care about what we do for them, whether we are working on a large property development or a small family problem. We need to get to know them as people rather than as simply as a piece of work. We also need to look at the way we deliver our services to ascertain if we truly are delivering what clients value.

6.3   What do clients value?

As we discussed in Chapter 2, most professionals still throw up their hands in horror at the suggestion of asking key clients what they think of their firms, their people and the services that they provide. However, as our clients are the ultimate judges of the quality of what we provide, the source of what additional services we should develop and at the end of the day, the future success of our organisations, it is essential that we carry out regular Client Service Audits.

Taking feedback from our clients is important as it allows us to tailor our services and identify future services. It also enables us to identify the types of clients we want to encourage and build into our future success. Every client is different and as a result, what is 'value for money' for one person will not be perceived as good value by another. However, as a minimum, all of our clients deserve to receive a quality professional service, delivering what they have asked for within the timescales we indicated and within the costs we agreed with them.

Some of the information this analysis produces will be positive, as clients can tell us a lot about what happens in other areas of our firms and what people say about us. They can also offer suggestions about what can be done better and most importantly, how services can be improved. As always, very simple aspects are important to them, for example, how friendly or helpful our support staff are or how well reception deals with them when they call into our offices. One facilities management consultants firm I know tells everyone in its formal presentations and website how expert it is in this service, yet any female client visiting its offices would have noticed that the doors in the ladies toilets do not shut properly!

Too often firms feel that clients buy from them on price alone. Yet, selling on price can create a number of difficulties, which include that:

1. the work may not be profitable,
2. the whole relationship is based on money, rather than value,
3. it devalues other aspects of the service delivery,
4. the professionals doing the work may feel undervalued,
5. it causes difficulties when the brief requires alteration,
6. it has a direct influence on future fees, and
7. it affects the firm's image and positioning in the marketplace.

It is important to remember that clients 'value' other aspects of the services they buy. Again, to appreciate this, we need to think that on many occasions, we will pay *over the odds* to secure something we need or particularly want. Clients make the same kind of decisions when choosing to employ their professional advisors.

So what criteria do they apply? Having listened to a wide range of clients, they all mention to me accessibility, value for money and pleasant and helpful support staff. They describe their frustration with not understanding what is involved in a piece of work, how long it will take and how much it will cost. They speak of professionals who talk much more than they listen, who focus on the process of what they do rather than the results they obtain, and being reactive rather than proactive. This feedback allows us to identify the core elements which form the bases of building valuable relationships with our clients. In summary, these include that we must:

1.   establish and agree their expectations,
2.   agree timescales, levels of service and costs,
3.   develop and retain their trust,
4.   be responsive to their needs,
5.   be good listeners,
6.   find proactive solutions to their problems, and
7.   deliver results not processes.

Let us now look at each of these seven elements in more detail.

6.3.1 Establish and agree clients' expectations

Too often clients come to us with totally unrealistic expectations of what is achievable – in terms of timescales, costs and/or outcomes. We do not have a magic wand that can make everything right for them or resolve complex matters without taking time, incurring costs and dealing with details.

Part of this lack of realism stems from lack of understanding of what individual professionals actually do to earn their fees. We need to think how little we know of other professions and their daily work demands. What do building surveyors do that is different from quantity surveyors? What do solicitors do that takes so much time and produces so much paperwork? What do accountants do other than sit in meetings? Clients are at an even greater disadvantage as they are not familiar with our language. Because of this, clear terms of engagement letters are vital. These must be written in simple language, dealing with the essentials of what we will do for our clients and how. In my experience, they often run to many pages of carefully drafted caveats and disclaimers, which may offer the potential of a strong case in the event of client complaints but are not likely to start from the premise of building trusting relationships.

Clients tell me that most of all they want clear initial explanations from their professionals about what is involved. Few clients are comfortable with being asked to write a blank cheque for intangible services, which they cannot test out in advance or make any objective assessment of the quality of the services being supplied. Firms should therefore develop handouts and flowcharts showing the process, anticipated timescales, who does what and what the client is expected to do.

6.3.2 Agree timescales, levels of service and costs

Clients therefore want us to advise them in direct and simple terms what is achievable, how long it will take and how much it will cost. If what they want is too time consuming or expensive, they want to know this upfront so that they can adjust their choice or select an alternative solution. They want the benefit of our expertise and advice to decide on options. Once they have been guided through this and made their choice, most clients are happy to let us get on and implement it. If matters go off course, they expect to be informed in good time to be able to adjust that choice. Over and above that, they want us to keep the end result of what they are trying to achieve in mind.

They want us to be *'sympathetic'* to their situation, not just provide surgically precise information, to show them that we care about what we do in general and what we are doing for them in particular. This once again highlights the importance of accessibility. Clients continue to complain about poor communications. With due respect to our professional brethren, some of us still use long-winded and complicated jargon. Similarly, the tone of much of our correspondence and emails can sound aggressive and/or arrogant.

When clients talk about accessibility, they mean having direct contact with someone who has up-to-date information about their file and can progress matters. I regularly hear of clients phoning in day after day without the courtesy of a return call. We seem to forget that in most cases, the matter is very important to our clients. Many still feel intimidated about phoning professionals. They may well wait beside the phone for a return call, thinking that they will be phoned back in 20 minutes. Yet, some professionals I talk to think that to phone people back within two days is acceptable. No wonder some clients become agitated.

They also want matters to be resolved with all possible speed – so that they can get the keys of their new property, access to their money or simply get on with their lives. For example, no one enjoys visiting the doctor, dentist or lawyer. They provide services that we would prefer not to use and prolonging the agony serves no one. Clients also need to be educated in what *we* expect from *them*. We do expect them to be up front and honest with us and not abuse our time or support staff. Giving them indications of timescales and when we need them to provide information or funds allows them to prepare accordingly. Clients, like most people, hate surprises. As a result, talking about money up front is vital.

(a)   Talking about money

Too often professionals avoid talking about money or if asked directly by the client, become hesitant and evasive. When I ask professionals to analyse why this happens, they come up with a variety of excuses. These range from:

- being too embarrassed,
- being afraid of the client's reaction,
- not understanding the basis of charging,
- being worried about quoting the wrong amount,
- needing time to think,
- being uncertain about the brief,
- not considering it to be their job, and
- afraid that it might damage or devalue the relationship.

In all of these, prior preparation and practice of such discussions will help. We must remember that commercial clients especially, often push us on the subject of money, to test how we will react. They argue that if we cannot talk comfortably about money with them, how well will we do it when acting for them? They see this therefore as a test of our competence.

Quite apart from not building our clients' trust in and respect for us, the practical consequences of not talking about money are considerable. These include:

- not getting the work at all as our competitors are better at it,

- that the client becomes frustrated or confused about likely costs,
- the work is started before costs are agreed,
- there are different perceptions about what is covered and what is not,
- it causes internal management problems,
- it causes later misunderstandings and problems with payment and level of fees,
- the client has no certainty of budget and feels 'unsure' about service levels, and
- overall it damages the working relationship.

All of these problems are significant and should be avoided as such misunderstandings and ambiguity undermines our ability to build trust. It is essential therefore to educate our people in how to talk about money in an informed and comfortable way. In my experience, this education is best done directly, through in-house training sessions.

6.3.3 Develop and retain trust

Clients do not know how to select their professional advisors. They often have no detailed understanding of what we do for them. Even the most sophisticated commercial clients talk of a '*leap of faith*' when it comes to instructing us. In other words, they have to make a judgement based on trust. As everyday life becomes even more complicated, clients have no real perception of the content of the service they are buying. They are forced more and more to cling to the intangible aspects of their buying decision – their confidence in our knowledge and reliability. We have discussed trust in some detail in Chapter 4. The same comments with regard to its fragility and intangibility apply here. Trust is nebulous and is based on intuition, backed up by personal recommendations from people we already trust.

Professionals also want client relationships to be based on trust. Most of us want to work with clients who trust us to get on with the job and who are loyal to our firms. Some of you will be saying that that is all in the past, and that I am being naive to think that such a relationship is possible. However, if we treat clients as though we do not trust them, covering our backs with detailed letters and defensive language, they will respond in kind. Ironically if we concentrate on developing a trusting relationship, we will become what our clients are asking of us – i.e. the proactive professional who thinks about what each client wants to achieve and gives their work priority. As a result, as discussed in Chapter 5, we need to be selective about the clients we take on.

Trust is therefore a very powerful tool in developing client relationships. However, there are some key aspects about it that we need to remember:

1. each side need to trust the other,
2. it requires openness and honesty,
3. it is particular to the individuals involved,
4. it takes time to develop, and
5. it can be destroyed easily.

I sometimes ask young professionals to work out how we develop trust with clients and how we lose trust. They find it an easy exercise to complete, commenting that what I have asked them to do is too simplistic. But that is exactly the issue. Developing trust is what *all* good professionals are committed to. To develop trust we need to be honest and upfront with clients about what we can and cannot do, stick to the timescales we have indicated and do what we said we would do. To lose trust, we need to avoid issues and break promises or undertakings we made to them.

Developing a trusting relationship brings benefits to us as well as the client. When clients trust us:

- we don't have to cover our backs,
- we can get on with what we need to do,
- they pay us without any problems, and
- they let us get on with our work.

The overall end result is that they will allow us some leeway as life is not always perfect!

6.3.4 Be responsive to their needs

We must be responsive to the needs of our clients. To achieve this, it is therefore important to see it from the client's perspective and think about how we feel when we go to seek personal advice from another professional. On many occasions, clients come to us:

- feeling unsure what to expect – how much it will cost, how long it will take, what does it mean,
- having heard *'awful'* stories about other people's bad experiences (we will remember that clients are three times as likely to tell people about their bad experiences than their good), and
- not wanting to come to see us at all because they have made a mistake, have avoided dealing with something, or through no fault of their own at all.

As a result, they may appear defensive, anxious, angry and distrustful. We need to be able to handle this behaviour, show them that we understand and have experience of their problems, explain what we need from them and develop their trust. One of the best ways of doing this is to spend time upfront listening to them.

6.3.5 Be good listeners

It is important to really listen to clients when they first come to see us. They may not always give us consistent information. Sometimes, they may appear to want to press ahead with some specific activity, when in fact, they want us to talk them out of it. Unfortunately, many professionals are poor listeners. We have a habit of scanning conversations, sorting and sifting as we go along. We tend to finish people's sentences for them, hurry them along and even interrupt. We quite often take notes. This can mean that when clients are talking to us about something they feel passionate about, they end up talking to the tops of our heads. So much for our eye contact! It is no wonder that professionals are often criticised for being poor communicators.

To appreciate how we may appear to our clients, it helps if we think again of other professionals outwith our own discipline. When we see our GP, think of how quickly he or she reaches for the prescription pad. We may wonder if we have been given enough time and attention to explain what we are really worried about. I am not suggesting that the GP has not done a professional job. We may well have come out of the surgery with the right solution to our problem but do we fully understand and appreciate that? Similarly, if we think about reading a building survey report on a house we want to buy for ourselves. Surveyors quite correctly focus on what is wrong with the house, but to a layman, a survey report often makes us feel that the house is in imminent danger of falling down.

We looked at the importance of listening in Chapter 4. Good listeners listen rather than talk. They look at us and appear to be paying attention to what we say. They wait for us to finish and then ask questions which show that they have listened to what we have told them. The opposite is equally true. Both sides are summarised in Table 6.3.5.

We need to develop our listening skills to allow clients to feel that they are working with people who fully understand them. For those of us with too much to do already, to suggest that we concentrate on spending even more time listening to clients must seem like an insane suggestion. However, if we spend time establishing what each client wants to achieve at the outset, this will allow us to focus on delivering that rather than wasting time at a later stage, altering our brief. This should then allow us to get on with the job with less interruptions and time-consuming back covering. Using technology to take the drudgery out of routine elements of our work will also free up our time.

6.3.6   Find proactive solutions to problems

In Chapter 4 we looked at the importance of solving internal problems. Clients also want us to solve their problems. Many professionals are trained to be technically skilled and adept at finding reasons *against* adopting a certain course of action. Few seem to understand the importance of also finding a practical

Table 6.3.5 Listening

Good listeners do	Good listeners do not
• Listen rather than talk • Maintain eye contact and positive body language • Let us finish • Make us feel important • Ask for clarification if they don't understand • Prompt us if we lose our train of thought • Empathise with us	• Talk about themselves • Fidget and look bored • Interrupt • Allow themselves to be interrupted • Make assumptions • Jump to conclusions • Sit in judgement of us

solution. For example, whilst many clients may have a legal remedy, the costs and time involved in pursuing this through the courts may not benefit the client in the long run. A more immediate out of court settlement may be better. Similarly, a client who wants to jump at what appears to be a financially lucrative property deal may need to be persuaded of the longer-term consequences of signing up to such a contract.

To be an effective problem solver requires the ability to:

- analyse an issue and identify possibilities,
- plan ahead and think dispassionately,
- gather accurate factual information,
- gain access to expert help and practical advice, both internally and externally,
- be open minded to suggestions, good at listening and learning,
- think innovatively and 'out of the box', and
- present solutions in a persuasive way.

Most clients want their professionals to take their problems away and fix them, not bother them with the details of what is involved and most importantly, progress matters with good speed. Many clients have little perception of, or indeed interest, in the technical details of what we do. This means that once we have established what *each* client wants, we should be able to get on with what we do without spending too much time explaining technical issues. I accept that, in some cases, we need to educate our clients about what is actually achievable for them and sometimes, we need the passage of time to allow clients to come to terms with the reality of their situation. However, in most other cases, clients simply want us to get on and do it.

They also want us to think ahead – to foresee potential problems and find ways of avoiding them before they arise. Few things annoy clients more than being told by their advisor that *'when we met initially six months ago, I thought that this issue would arise'*. It is our job to use our experience to be proactive rather than reactive, and as a result, prevent that situation arising.

6.3.7 Deliver results not processes

Technology continues to provide huge potential to remove the drudgery of routine client work. It allows us to standardise a lot of what we do and at the same time, tailor the services to individual clients. In other words, it allows us to drive down the cost of producing the work and concentrate on the elements that the clients value i.e. direct contact with their professional advisor.

Some firms, however, have forgotten the nature of the services clients want. Clients want us to provide support rather than paperwork. Introducing standard procedures for what we do is fine if we remember that we still act for people not just file numbers. For example, buying a house is regarded as generating almost as high stress levels as a divorce. I know it often appears that all house purchase clients are agitated – but in fact they are!

IT also provides the opportunity to progress work faster as less time is needed on drafting and checking. The quicker we can progress the project to a successful conclusion, the quicker we will get paid and the happier our clients will be. As a result, we need to change *where* we spend our time, moving from routine document producing to adding value to the client relationship – using our skills and experience to devise an effective solution to his or her problems.

Not all clients value the same thing – some value our detailed and intricate specialist advice, others our pragmatic, problem-solving approach. That is what makes our work exciting and challenging. We need to be chameleons, matching clients with particular types of people within our firms to deliver what each client wants. For example, overly busy clients want us to take away the details, sort them out and *not* send them endless reams of paperwork. Commercial clients want their deals done within agreed timescales, input from us about better options and for us to co-ordinate all of other professionals involved.

Clients want us to be innovative in how we deal with their work. They pay us for our ability to find a practical result. They also want us to take a commercial view of what can be done, rather than stick slavishly to the 'safe' answer. Being proactive requires that we have the time to plan ahead – time to sit back and look at what can be achieved. However, most of us spend too much time doing and not enough time thinking. We need to devise ways of providing quicker and/or better solutions as this allows us to show clients that we care about resolving the situation. When we do that, we build a reputation for delivering good results. It also allows us to concentrate on what we enjoy doing.

We now need to look at the application of what we have learned about our clients and what they value in the context of cross selling to existing clients and winning new clients.

6.4   Implementing Cross Selling

Nearly every professional firm speaks of the importance of cross selling its full range of services to clients, yet very few firms achieve it in practice. However, the strategy of cross selling is sound as the effort and time it takes to attract new clients away from their existing professional advisors is considerable. It is much easier to sell new services to existing clients who already appreciate the quality of what we provide to them. We already understand these clients and what they value, and therefore can focus on explaining the benefits our additional services will bring them.

It will also bring significant benefits to our firms, which include:

- increased sales, the potential to maximise the use of existing overheads, and increase profit margins,
- improvements in communications and inter-departmental understanding,
- improvements in consistency and quality of service, and
- identification and sharing of best practice.

Many of us are all too familiar with the problems associated with selling professional services. Quite apart from the difficulties of selling something intangible, our clients often do not want to buy from us in the first place, seeing our service as a necessary evil. Also, professionals are deeply uncomfortable with the concept of 'selling', and even perceive it as something inherently unprofessional. Even when professionals are brave enough to try to introduce clients to other parts of their firms, it can go wrong. When work is referred to another professional or department, the client may not enjoy the experience, which will reflect badly on the professional making the original referral.

Given that the strategy of cross selling is correct, how can we overcome these problems and put it into practice?

First of all we need to educate our clients about our services and their benefits.

We need to support our clients through the crossover process and make sure that internally, we reward people who make it happen.

6.4.1 Educate our clients

As outlined earlier, most clients have difficulty understanding what professionals actually do. As a result, we need to start by educating clients about the range of services we provide. By this, I mean that we need to give them basic information about what we do, and most importantly, what benefits that will bring to them. The best professional brochures and web sites achieve this by providing illustrations, sometimes by way of case studies or stories of the successes these firms have achieved for their clients.

Many professionals seem to have become incapable of seeing it from the client's perspective. As a result, when asked to define the benefits of their services, they talk a lot about the technical content of what they do. However, we must be able to define the benefits of our services from the client's point of view. As we have already discussed, most clients value speed of response and that their professionals concentrate on delivering results. As a result, we need to focus on promoting those aspects rather than telling clients how expert we are. For example, the benefits of our litigation or landlord and tenant department should not describe the expertise of our partners but should instead illustrate our speedy resolution of what appear to clients as being insurmountable difficulties. Yes, I can hear my colleagues commenting that that is easy to say but very difficult to achieve, but that is the point I am making. To earn high quality fees and win high quality clients and work, we need to be able to do what many other professionals cannot.

It is worthwhile stopping at this point to reflect on what we say in our websites, formal presentations and brochures. Are we telling the clients how important we are or are we telling them what we can *do* for them? It is essential to develop all our communications to existing and new clients with this orientation in mind.

To focus on what our clients value, it is essential to be able to answer these three questions:

1.   What services and products do we offer to clients?
2.   What are the features of these (i.e. what distinguishes them from what

our competitors are offering)? and

3.   What benefits do our clients gain from them?

For example, rather than talk about the process of facilities management, we should highlight the benefits it brings. For our client's Finance Director, it brings certainty of budgets and cash flow, no surprises and no embarrassment at Board meetings when he or she has to ask for exceptional funds to pay for some major building repair. It also ensures that capital assets maintain their value year on year.

6.4.2 Hand holding is not a waste of time

Once we have ascertained what our clients want and what they will want from us in the future, we can then introduce new services to them. This is a very important stage in the relationship and must be handled with care. Clients, like most people, are resistant to change. They do not like having to get to know another professional and will not take it well if they have to explain themselves to other people within our firm, as they will expect quite rightly, that the handing over of details about their background should already have been made.

Retaining contact with them after the handover is essential. Too often, the referring professional hands clients over without any attempt to keep in touch with them. Too often, the new professional keeps the referring professional out of the communication loop. This causes professional and client problems on all sides, which include:

1.   clients feel abandoned and forced to build the new relationship themselves,
2.   the referring professional feels resentful that he or she has been taken for granted,
3.   existing client relationships becomes vulnerable as clients struggle to get to terms with the dynamics of the new relationship, and
4.   particular background knowledge of the clients' situation may be missed which can cause professional indemnity problems later on.

On one occasion, I nearly lost an important client of mine as a result of referring him to a partner in another office. After making the introduction and attending their initial introductory meeting, I was kept in the dark about what was happening. When I phoned the client for a routine chat a couple of months later, he was less than civil to me as he had just received a large bill from my colleague which I knew nothing about and which he considered was outrageously high when in his view, little had been achieved.

It is therefore essential to keep all three sides of the referral triangle in touch with each other as the new relationship develops.

Initially at least, the client will tend to check out the new service or advice with the original professional. As a result, he or she should be kept informed about developments *in advance* of the client to make sure that the advice or approach will be acceptable to the client. This may not look cost effective in the short term but it will pay dividends in the long term by developing a strong and cohesive relationship, both internally and externally.

6.4.3   Make sure we reward cross selling

Professionals are reluctant to get involved in anything that is described as *'selling'*. They see it as unprofessional and not what they should be asked to do. Yet, many of them talk about the importance of client care and delivering high quality professional service. It is important therefore to build on that inherent commitment to client relationships rather than put professionals off the concept by talking about increasing their selling skills. Cross selling (or more accurately cross referrals) is about developing and *deepening* existing relationships with clients. Once professionals see it from that perspective, it is much easier to encourage them to do it.

We need to ensure that our structure and culture supports that aim. Too often, firms specify the importance of cross selling in their business or marketing plan yet operationally set fee and time targets which actively discourage it. Professionals and clients alike must believe in the quality of *all* of the services we provide and of *all* of the people providing it. People must know and value each other as cross selling will not be achieved in an atmosphere of distrust and resentment. As a result, we need to educate each other about what we do, through cross-departmental in-house presentations and promoting examples of successful cross selling. We need to ensure that we follow through by developing ways to reward the people who implement it. These could include recognition for the introduction to the new service or a percentage reward on the fee recovered. We also need to ensure that people and departments trust each other and are willing to share clients.

Implementing successful cross selling is one of the core elements of sustainable business growth. We know our existing clients and what they value. We should build on this and expand the range of support we provide to them. Clients choose us because they trust our professional judgement and us. It is important to maintain and not damage that connection. Cross selling implies that we trust the professional we refer our client on to and that the client will benefit from that additional service. We need to believe in the value that we can provide to our clients.

We now need to move on and look at the concept of 'value-based' selling in more detail.

6.5   Value-based selling to win new clients

'Value-based' selling has become the vogue for many professional firms. Quite correctly, it is argued that clients will buy our services if we focus on the value that we bring to them. However, as we outlined above, if we place too much emphasis on the word 'selling', we estrange a lot of professionals from becoming involved in the process.

Some of their resistance comes from the use of the word 'selling' as it conjures up pictures of second-hand car or time-share sales pitches. They argue that it is not our job to sell our services, rather it is for our clients to come to us and ask us to provide our services to them. However, given that clients continue to be vague about what we can do to help them, we need to be able to explain what we can do for them. Value-based selling by definition focuses on 'values'. However, for most of us working directly with clients and other professionals, many of the skills are similar. As we have already established, it is our job to find out what is valuable to our clients and then find ways of delivering that value through our service.

We need to find out as much as we can about the potential new client and what that client is likely to want and need from professional advisors. We must plan our presentation to them, decide whether it should be formal or informal, who will be involved from both sides, its content and how long it should take. Often, we may only have a short space of time in the constraints of a formal presentation to get our message across in a way that the potential client is able to distinguish us from other presenters and, most importantly, feel that they could work with us in the future. We need to both ask and answer questions and listen to what is said. Over and above all of this, we need to show that we are passionate about what we do.

In summary, the key skills we need to harness include the ability to:

1.   source and analyse information,
2.   forward plan and structure words and thoughts,
3.   communicate strongly and develop empathy,
4.   effectively question, probe and listen,
5.   deal with challenges and objections, and
6.   show that we care about what we do.

It is worthwhile putting professionals through some internal training on this 'sales' process to overcome their initial resistance to the whole concept. As a result, we must never call it 'sales training' as this puts professionals off from the outset. Many a time, I have been asked to deliver this type of training and had to spend half of the first morning persuading people that they are not being asked to become salespeople. Once we get over that initial hurdle and they realise that what we are offering will benefit their clients and improve their service delivery, they enjoy the session.

If we focus on the six skills outlined above, most professionals will discover that the process of selling should give good professionals little concern or problems as we *already have these skills*. For example, what good professional cannot source and analyse information? Is not able to forward plan and structure words and thoughts? This provides reassurance that what we are asking people to do is not alien to them or against their professional values. What we are asking them to do is to focus on what the client wants and needs.

Let us now look at this in the context of formal presentations or pitches.

6.5.1 Winning pitches

Clients can only appreciate what we do for them by what they directly experience. As a result, to win a pitch for work, we need to be able to contextualise what we will provide – by showing them that we have expertise in and experience of their particular situation. In addition, we need to start to build a working relationship. At the end of the day, clients will have to make a personal judgement about whether to use us or not. We have already established the importance that trust plays in the clients' selection process. As we have discussed clients want to work with people who understand them and are focused on solutions. Finally, clients want their professionals to listen to them. Too often when making formal presentations, professionals do all of the talking and expect the clients to be impressed by this. Clients however, would prefer to be listened to rather than talked at, even when it comes to formal pitches.

(a)   Contextualise what we do

Many professional brochures and web sites tell us how important these firms are – for example, that they have offices in 15 cities in Europe or that they employ 200 people. This generates a *'so what'* response in clients – *'so what does that mean for me?'* Clients can become cynical about expensive offices, web sites and staff and wonder if they will be expected to pay for all of these in the fees we charge. Quoting our hourly rates at them merely confirms that we charge by the hour rather than by the results we achieve. Clients are much more interested in finding out whether the firm has experience of their particular situation and what success it has achieved for other clients.

It has become fashionable to present formal pitches using PowerPoint software. This allows firms to develop template introductions about themselves and their services. However, many clients now complain of *'PowerPoint fatigue'*, where teams of professionals spend 40 minutes or an hour talking at them, showing no regard for the clients' business or any understanding of their situation. Clients notice when there has been little pre-thought or preparation and often find it difficult to differentiate one group of presenters from another.

Some firms do rehearse and practice their presentations but many do not, thinking that they will *'wing it'* on the day, as the time and effort involved in preparation is costly. As a result, it is essential to focus on formal presentations which are worth this investment. One of my clients accepted any and every opportunity to pitch for work, with the result that they won one in ten pitches. They estimated that, including preparation and travel time, each pitch cost them about £4000, with the result that the one piece of work they did win had to generate £36,000 of profit to break even. By shifting their emphasis and concentrating on targeting clients where they can build a valuable relationship, they now win one pitch in three.

It is important to think through the content of the presentation. With limited time, it is essential to make it direct and straightforward, avoiding jargon. Depending on the client, using humour can be a valuable way of getting our message across. One firm of surveyors, pitching for a project where teamwork was vital, simply showed three slides illustrating great cartoon teams.

It is also important to illustrate to the client what we can *actually* do by offering a couple of options of how the project would be tackled. This allows us to show our understanding of and experience in their situation, as well as illustrate that we are prepared to invest time in these particular clients up front.

In presentations, as with promotional material, it is essential to focus on the features and benefits of what we offer. Rather than tell clients that '*we have 200 staff based in 15 offices around the world*', we need to tell them what features differentiate us from our competitors and what benefits we can bring to our clients. We need to be able to *prove* that we 'add value' rather than simply *say* that we do, by providing real life examples of what we have actually achieved.

As discussed before, whether we trust a person is based on our instinct checked against our subsequent experience. In formal presentations, the key element is therefore to provide sufficient illustrations of what we have achieved for other clients to allow potential new clients to make that choice. Stories about the firm and client projects are an excellent way of achieving this (see below).

Knowing who we are presenting to is vital. If, for example, the selection panel includes the Finance Director, he or she is likely to value professionals who minimise risk and deliver certainty. If we can provide examples of bringing the project through on time or where we directly reduced risk, that Director will want to work with us.

Formal pitches by definition can become too formal with clients struggling to see the people behind the presentation. It is important therefore to keep the pitch short and to the point and then sit down and let the clients speak.

(b)   Listen to them

In general, professionals tend to talk rather than listen, with clients complaining about our inability to communicate effectively. As a result, we need to be very careful about how much we talk, as listening to clients allows us to find out what is important to them and what they are looking for from their professionals. Questions from clients should be encouraged and prepared for and not something to avoid at all costs. Instead they should be seen as evidence that the client is interested enough to be part of the discussion. In many cases, we can second-guess the likely objections that will be raised, for example:

*   *'In what way are you different from firm X?'*
*   *'How can you add value?'*
*   *'Why are you so expensive?'*

We should anticipate the questions, be proactive about them and have our answers ready.

Clients also want to hear their professionals say that they *want* to work with them, yet many firms do not include that in their pitch. This may to us appear to be stating the obvious (as why else would we be here and have put all this effort into being here?) but in the clients' view, it still needs to be said.

In summary, there are a number of crucial stages to achieving a successful formal presentation. These include:

1.   preparing fully for any formal presentation, including the background to the client, their brief, their overall objective and the impact this project will have on their business,
2.   thinking through whether a formal presentation is the best option as many clients would prefer informality,
3.   finding out who will attend the presentation,
4.   tailoring the presentation to show that we understand their problems and using practical examples demonstrate what we can achieve for them,
5.   using stories to contextualise and illustrate what we do, demonstrate our values and how we add value,
6.   keeping it short and to the point,
7.   building in time to listen to the clients proving that we are confident that we can take any questions they have,

8.   having some specific questions for them to illustrate that we have thought about them and their challenges,

9.   if possible, offering them a number of options as this bypasses the first stage of clients asking themselves '*Should we use them?*' to the second stage of asking '*How can we use them?*', and

10.   saying that we want to work with them!

The *process* of successful formal presentations is important with each of these stages fully addressed. It is essential never to make assumptions and hope that we can '*wing it*' on the day as lack of preparation always shows. Finally it is important not to assume that formal presentations are always the best way to convince a potential client. Some clients would prefer informality.

6.5.2 Informal presentations

Informal presentations to clients happen every time we meet and talk to them. In essence, every meeting with contacts and potential new clients is an opportunity to 'pitch' for work. As always it is important to have some structure to what we are trying to achieve.

As clients choose us because they like us as people, most of us have the opportunity to talk to potential new clients and contacts on a daily basis as we go about our work. More formally, it is important to choose the type of networking that we are comfortable with. Some people prefer lunches or dinners where they can chat pleasantly to a small group of people. Other people can successfully '*work a room*' without knowing anyone there and leave a trail of business cards behind them. Others do most of their client development on the golf course, tennis courts or gym.

In any of these situations, it is impossible to talk in too much detail about what our firms offer without appearing '*too pushy*'. However, what we can always do is tell a story.

6.5.3 The importance of stories

Stories are an important part of both formal and informal presentations. Indeed, they are an essential part of developing client relationships generally. Stories are important for a number of reasons. They allow us to:

- illustrate our values and what is important to us,
- show what differentiates us from our competitors,
- put what we do in a context that the client can understand,
- demonstrate in a tangible way that our services can bring real and practical benefits,
- illustrate our specialist knowledge in the context of their particular situation, and
- overall help clients understand better what we do.

They also allow us to be remembered in a distinctive way – and talked about to other (potential) clients. They are therefore powerful tools in building long-term relationships.

From the client management point of view, they also are an excellent solution to telling clients they are wrong without directly confronting them. For example, telling a client about another client in a similar situation who ended up with a bad result because of pursuing a certain line, is an easier way of getting that message across. However, there is one aspect of using stories that has to be borne in mind at all times. Most clients hate to think that we would be telling such stories about them to other clients. Clients therefore pick up immediately on any breach of confidentiality. It is essential therefore not to use actual names or give any information that would allow the client situation to be identified.

6.6   Marketing and branding

So far in this Chapter, we have focused on our clients and what they value. I have not mentioned the word 'marketing' or 'branding'. Based on my experience of being personally responsible for business development in my firm and from working with senior management teams, too often the person in charge of marketing is expected to wave a magic wand, spend the marketing budget on advertisements and promotional literature, develop a brand and as a result, new clients will flood in. However, new business generation is the responsibility of the whole firm, from the receptionist who may take the initial enquiry to the fee-earner that is asked to complete the new project.

Most of us now accept that selling and branding professional services is not that easy. Our 'products' are intangible and vary depending on our client sector or service. Our clients buy us because of intangible reasons, for example, that they trust the individual they work with. Clients in general continue to find difficulty in distinguishing what we do. The only way they can chose is on the basis of firstly, *personal* recommendations and secondly, whether they *like* the firm.

It is therefore essential to promote our personality, our values and our distinctiveness in our websites, literature, formal presentations and stories. It is equally important for the clients to experience that same personality and culture when they speak to us, meet with us and visit us. This must be built into our recruitment and training programmes as that is the essence of branding for professional service organisations.

Conclusions

Building valuable relationships with our clients forces us to focus on the long term. As a result, we need to ensure that our firm delivers services in the way that our clients value. This requires that we listen and respond to them, as well as concentrate on achieving results in as short a time scale as possible.

Cross referrals and value-based selling are important tools for successful client and firm development. The skills required are no different from those of good professionals who are able to communicate effectively. It is important to provide reassurance that *'selling'* is not unprofessional and provide training to reinforce that.

Business development includes both formal and informal presentations, telling stories and maximising our brand.

Key Action Points

1. deliver exceptional service consistently throughout the firm
2. focus on what clients' value, not on price
3. become comfortable with talking about money
4. always demonstrate to clients that we have listened to them
5. find proactive solutions not more problems
6. reward cross selling and cross referrals
7. do not talk too much in formal presentations
8. develop some powerful success stories about our firm

7

CHOOSING THE CORRECT DEVELOPMENT OPTION

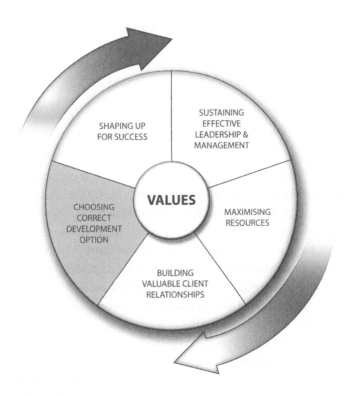

7.1   Introduction

In Chapter 2, we considered the importance of strategic thinking, looked the choices available to professional firms and how we could put these into practice. In this Chapter, we will develop these themes and identify how to select and implement our correct strategic option.

As we have discussed before, it is important to constantly review and check our response to market changes as new trends and options appear. Chapter 3 highlighted a number of these trends and current management models. In this Chapter, we will put these into the context of our firms, test their effect and identify ways of tackling them.

Some of us will already be familiar with and have successfully implemented a number of the strategies. These may have included growing the firm organically by expanding and cross selling the range of services provided to existing clients. Some of us will have achieved accelerated growth through planned mergers and joint ventures with other firms. Some may have gone further and hived off part of our services into alternative trading structures, branded or identified differently from our mainstream activities. The correct choice is up to us to make. To do so we need to know what we want to achieve.

7.2   Know what we want to achieve

Strategic options for professional service firms are and continue to be, limited by the trading structure they adopt. Partnerships, by their nature, depend on resources contributed by its partners with third party funding based on secured and unsecured borrowings. To move away from these restrictions, some professionals have adopted limited liability structure. In my experience, this has sometimes brought with it tensions between ownership and rewarding non-owners who contribute significantly to financial success. Diversification as an option is also difficult to achieve, as most professional firms are restricted both operationally and strategically by the rules of their professional bodies. Whilst some multi-discipline functions are possible for some professions, differences in styles of approach to client service and feeing can cause practical and cultural problems. As a result, we are often constrained in our range of strategic options and have to think innovatively about how we will achieve them. This reinforces our premise that successful firms are those that *implement* strategies rather than simply talk about them.

In my experience, the implementation of many strategies fails as a result of a clash between the values of the partners and the values created by the strategic choice. For example, if we have a high value of independence, we are unlikely to succeed with an accelerated growth strategy where our firm opts to become part of a much larger entity. As always, it is essential to check our choice with our core values. I often see illustrations of this difficulty – where the two original firms have come together with different values and drivers. One firm may have a high driver of professional expertise and the other, a commercial approach to client advice. Partners on both sides begin to resent the *'pushy'* approach of one group or the *'intellectual'* style of the other. Their management struggles to reach agreement on basic issues, such as charge out rates or fee levels, people are accused of *'cutting corners'* or being *'too long-winded'* and staff continue to see an *'us and them'* culture. After a few years of unhappiness, such firms often demerge, with partners exhausted, clients confused and profitability and reputation damaged.

Strategic choices follow three distinct stages. We need to address:

1.   what we want to achieve in the short, medium and long term, based on our values, resources and analysis of the current and future marketplace,
2.   the identification and development of what options are available and fit with our values, resources and market, and
3.   the selection and implementation of these options.

Let us start with stage one. Firstly, we need to refer back to our Business Plan to identify our short, medium and long-term objectives. We already know our values. We also need to ensure that we have the potential resource base to implement what we want to do. Then we need to tackle our analysis of the marketplace.

7.3   Stage 1 Market analysis

Sometimes it seems that we are completely controlled by the market, blown hither and thither by the winds of change. We always seem to need more staff of one type of work and less of another. And everyone has to work quicker and quicker. As a result, we need to take control and anchor ourselves to what we want to achieve. To do this, we must develop the discipline to take time to think and forward plan. In Chapter 3, we developed a list of key changes that have influenced professionals over the past ten years. These included that our clients have become much more demanding of us, that traditional areas of fee income have been driven down and that the professions are suffering from increased external regulation. We also considered in detail a number of strategic shifts applicable to the professional sector in particular. These included continually adding value to our client service delivery as providing high quality professional services is the minimum that clients now demand, and the need to focus on profitability and changing the way we work. We must always be responsive to changes in the market and as a result, constantly review and adjust our trading and operational structures.

It is important to use a structure for our analysis of the marketplace, such as Porter's 5 Forces Model (1980). This allows organisations to determine the marketplace pressures acting upon it by analysing the impact of a number of external factors. I have adapted Porter's model to include six headings rather than five by adding a new heading of 'quality people' to reflect its strategic importance for professional service organisations. We therefore need to apply our market knowledge to considering how vulnerable we are to:

1.   the power and influence of our clients,
2.   our supply of quality staff,
3.   our suppliers,
4.   our indirect competitors,
5.   our direct competitors, and
6.   the risk of substitute services.

Therefore if we combine the Model with the market trend analysis we completed in Chapter 3, we can interpret Porter's Model as detailed in Table 7.3.

This analysis therefore allows us to develop and refine our strategic response. This in turn informs our operational priorities. For example, we can identify that the key issues for the professional sector *in general* are the need to actively manage our clients, quality people, dependence on IT, differentiation from our competitors, and how we deliver our services. If we are able to differentiate ourselves and keep our clients loyal, we will be able to keep our direct competitors at bay. If we are able to retain our quality people, we will be able to deliver a consistently high quality service and retain key clients.

We will now move on to consider the effect of these trends in the particular context of individual firms.

Table 7.3 Porter's Model Analysis

FORCE	ANALYSIS
CLIENTS	The power and influence of our **clients** continue to increase. Clients come to us because they need our help. If we do not respond to this need in a way they think offers accessibility and good value, other professionals will capture them. Given that levels of business activity always fluctuate, it is vitally important to build long term-relationships with our quality clients.
QUALITY PEOPLE	Our supply of **quality people** is under pressure. There may be more people in the market, but many do not have the skills or technical knowledge we need. Expert IT and training managers are very difficult to find. Mobility of people, including senior partners and whole teams, is on the increase and must be managed in a positive way.
SUPPLIERS	As we become more and more dependent on information technology, our vulnerability to IT **suppliers,** in particular, is on the increase.
INDIRECT COMPETITORS	The threat of **indirect competitors** for high risk work seems to be lessening because of the current decline in high volume, high fee work. Lower level, more routine work is being targeted by mass providers.
DIRECT COMPETITORS	There continues to be too many professional firms chasing too few quality clients. As a result, there is an ongoing need to stand our ground against **direct competition** as we all scramble for high quality work.
SUBSTITUTE SERVICES	The threat of **substitute services** continues with software developments, changes in reserved areas and clients more inclined to do things for themselves.

7.3.1 Application to our own firm

Most of the information about market trends can be readily gathered through working with banks, other professionals and our clients. We need to take this information, analyse it and assess our options. This exercise does not have to be too time consuming. We could spend an hour jotting down our thoughts, rationalising them, sorting them into some kind of structure and prioritising them. Those trends which are not important to us and which we have no control over, we can dismiss. Those which are important, we need to respond to. Those we have control over, we need to tackle. The essential response to all of this analysis is to be continually aware and flexible.

It is sometimes easier to see clues about what is happening in practice by analysing shifts in our fee income, for example, design work versus project management, divorce versus mediation, and audit versus forensic work. Once we have identified these, we need to ensure that we can respond to them. Do we have the right shape and structure to address these shifts? Too often young professionals have become specialised early on in their careers with the result that they do not have transferable skills. Many professional firms continue to migrate towards the very large or the very small. Where are we positioned? Are we middle-sized and apparently vulnerable? Are we too big to change our department structure quickly? As a small firm, do we have sufficient resources?

7.3.2   Use what clients want and value

We have talked already about the importance of taking client feedback and asking them what services they will want from us in the future. Delivering value in a way that clients see differentiates us from our competitors provides us with our competitive advantage.

It is equally important to look at changes in demography and client skills. For example, clients are becoming more computer literate and using the Internet to source information and services. In many cases, we can learn from our clients about how they want to access us, for example, through email, often outwith normal business hours. Clients also have access to more information but are often not, as a result, better informed. Indeed, the opposite may occur as they become more confused and need professional help to guide them through the morass of regulations or choices available to them. Some firms have responded to this by providing their clients with direct access to their Intranets, where summaries of sector or client specific information are available.

7.3.3 Focus on the long term

It is essential to take a longer term view rather than simply focus on the short term. We may need to invest in our resource base through developing new skills, expanding our pool of quality people, designing new software and support systems and/or increasing our capital base. We may need to move away from some clients or sectors, which have simply become unprofitable, because of downward pressure on fees and/or increased competition.

This in turn may require us to change our internal structure, by increasing or decreasing the number of client service departments and/or recruiting people with specialist skills. It may require us to change our trading structure, moving to limited liability partnership or expanding geographically. It is essential not to become too internally focused. We need to be able to access outside advice and ideas of what works in other firms or locations.

It is worthwhile at this point to remember the importance of values and their influence on our strategic choice. We must not seek to implement a strategy that undermines our core values. I will use the option of Multi Discipline Partnerships (MDPs) to illustrate this point.

MDPs offer a multi-discipline structure, with formal links to other types of professions, such as accountants and lawyers. Whilst employing other professionals in-house seems to suit some people and organisations, MDPs at the time of writing have been less successful. Quite apart from the impact of the Anderson network break up on law firms associated with it, tensions seem to exist between the different professions. In theory, such tensions should not exist as there is commonality of core professional values. However, in my experience, there seem to be a difference in *emphasis* between the professions. For example, I have worked with an established MDP of surveyors and architects and even with people who work together on a daily basis in the same office and over a period of years, different approaches to client service and delivery exist. How much more difficult that must be when people from different professional backgrounds work in different offices and different cities?

This results in a reluctance to share work and clients. Professionals will only refer important clients to colleagues they trust to deal with these clients in the same way they do. As we have discussed before such referrals do not happen simply because our firms are in association with each other. Indeed it often does not happen even when partners are in the same original firm!

In addition, it is not even clear that our clients and the marketplace support such a strategy. In my experience, commercial clients do not seem to see significant advantages to it, preferring to pick specialist advisors in different service and geographical areas. Given all of this, it would appear to me likely that with a limited market demand and increased regulation, we will continue to see a shift away from MDP structures.

7.4   Stage 2 Identifying and developing options

As I mentioned at the outset, it is important to match the strategy selected, first and foremost, with our values. As a result, if considering a merger, amalgamation or addition of new partners or teams, we also need to identify and agree with *their* values. It is unlikely that there will be an exact match but there *must* be some overlap. For example, one firm may have integrity, openness and profitability. The other may have profitability, pragmatism and fun. Both sets must be discussed collectively and core values common to both agreed. This Value exercise is essential and must involve all existing and potential partners as it provides a good opportunity for discussion and getting to know each other. Only *after* agreement has been reached, should further progress on the merger take place. The statistics (Marks & Mirvis 1998 p3) for successful mergers are very poor with less than 25% succeeding. Again and again, their failure comes down to clashes of cultures. For example, one client of mine took on a complete service team from a firm that had split up. They assumed that as they were an established and successful group, they would know how to behave and what to do. Yet, the managing partner told me that his time was being 'leeched away' dealing with behavioural issues of the new people as they *'simply seemed unable to fit in'*.

In Chapter 2, I argued that we trust people who share our values. Trust is essential for any new business venture as apart from the potential damage to our image and reputation, no amalgamation or merger ever goes smoothly. One of my clients identified a partner to expand their geographical base. They told me they *'liked'* the people in the other firm and felt that they could work with them. Just prior to their formal merger, their accountants found a difference in approach being taken between the two firms that fundamentally altered the capital base of one of them. Because they felt they could trust each other they went ahead regardless and allowed the finances to be sorted out later.

Once our values have been established, we can begin the process of selection of our strategy. In simple terms, we can grow bigger, remain the same or get smaller. It is essential to distinguish between turnover and profitability. In all three cases, profitability must increase or remain constant. In my view, turnover size is largely irrelevant as it is possible for smaller firms to be as profitable as larger ones particularly if they choose the right strategy.

I can illustrate this point with a story about one large surveying practice I was asked to help. It had adopted an accelerated growth by turnover. The partners 'bought' work at any price regardless of profit margins with clients promised anything to win the work. They pursued mergers and joint ventures across countries and continents. I was asked to facilitate the equity partners' business session, where I could see the tension around the room and the mistrust on many partners' faces – people who hardly knew each other. One year later the cracks in its operations were showing. Staff were unhappy, unable to meet the promises that had been made to clients and feeling undervalued doing work on a low fee base. Clients were unhappy, having been made promises that had not been kept, and felt taken advantage of and let down. Partners were being asked to put in more capital to feed the enormous overheads that had been created. Their management skills were stretched trying to run a global practice. They had not achieved economies of scale and had little idea of the skill base or personnel they had acquired through their various mergers and acquisitions. Two years later, in what had been a growing and buoyant market, they were in serious trouble with good people leaving, cash flow a major issue and their reputation in trouble.

It is important therefore to think through all of the implications of a strategic choice. We need to explore possible options, debate and adjust them until we develop one that suits us and matches our values, resources and market potential. It must also fit with our management skills. To achieve this mix may not be easy. If it was, most of our competitors would be doing it already. As a result, we need to look at ways of thinking differently about what to choose and how to implement it.

7.4.1 Innovative thinking

To achieve this, we must indulge in some innovative thinking. This can seem a scary concept for traditionally risk adverse professionals but we discussed the growing importance of innovation in Chapter 3. The essential element in creativity is in the practical application of the idea – not the idea itself. Accordingly, we need to include both logical (left) brain and creative (right) brain people in developing options.

As advocated in Chapter 2, I would suggest setting up a Strategy Group or allocate this responsibility to one key individual. Some firms call this their Strategy Board, Business Development Committee or Idea Generation Department. Their remit will be determined by the terms of their appointment and the strategy selected. They should concentrate on that remit and not interfere with operational management. In my experience, it is essential that that point be established from the outset as otherwise the Strategy Group will deliberately or accidentally drift into other areas. They should be tasked with a specific project, such as developing a new client product, within an agreed timeframe of not more than six months. The time frame must be kept tight to keep people focused on delivering an end result.

Whatever grouping of people we use, it is important to mix left and right brains as early as possible as they have to learn to work together and respect each other. They should be allowed to 'play' with some ideas, and then see what would work in practice. There are a number of traditional tools that can be used to encourage creative thinking, for example, Royal Dutch/Shell's Scenario Planning (for an excellent summation of this process see De Geus, 1999, Chapter 3), and the Disney Strategy (for a summary see Molden, 2001, Chapter 21). It is important to choose and use whichever tool we find most comfortable.

I tend to use a mixture of right brain activities as I am naturally a very logical, left-brained thinker. This is probably due to my training as a lawyer, yet when I became Business Development Partner for my amalgamated firm, I suddenly was expected to come up with new ideas. I discovered much to my surprise that I was able to be creative, to '*think out of the box*', and more importantly, work out how such ideas could be translated into practice. Since then, I have developed a range of ways of achieving this left and right brain balance. When overwhelmed with lists and words, I often draw a picture of what I want to achieve. I use mind mapping (Buzan, 1993) when I am confused by a number of ideas, using this technique to work out priorities and linkages. Using both sides of our brains is important. For example, when writing my first book, I became bogged down in the reams of words and pages. To re-energise myself and encapsulate what I wanted to achieve, I commissioned a series of cartoons.

We also need to follow our instincts rather than follow logic all of the time (see comments on Emotional Intelligence in Chapter 3). This illustrates that sometimes the right side of our brain comes up with the right solutions without any logical basis for them. Being innovative is what gives us competitive advantage. We need to release the time and the energy to indulge ourselves in some 'silly ideas' and thoughts. As a result, we should spend time every week *away* from our desks and computers.

7.4.2 Expansion as an option?

Some people may have thought of missing out this Chapter completely, arguing to themselves that their firm is fine the size it is. This may indeed be the case at this moment in time. However, as we have demonstrated, there are a number of significant trends influencing the professional sector that are ignored at our peril. For example, clients are increasingly demanding of their professionals and some work that historically was profitable is no longer cost effective. As a result, we need to constantly stop and assess the type of work we do and how we do it. We can all think of firms who have lost their position in the marketplace dramatically and quickly. We simply cannot afford to assume that what has worked for us in the past will continue to work for us in the future. One way of tackling this is to look at market expansion.

Expanding our business horizons is important for a number of reasons. First of all, many of us operate in niche markets. These markets are limited and vulnerable to new competitors coming into it, changing the way our services are delivered and/or driving down prices. Secondly, we can become too comfortable in our professional niches and fail to look outside to see what changes will have a direct impact on us. None of us can afford the luxury of assuming that what makes us successful now will continue to make us successful in the future. Being niche tends to make us 'narrow'. We may excel at what we do but we may miss some external factor that will damage us in the future. Too often I deal with clients who have simply not noticed what is happening around them. For example, many professions have lost their *'cash cows'* – their core areas of profitable work. Perhaps most importantly of all, our commercial clients demand that we can help them trade in an increasingly global market. Expansion is therefore a relevant consideration. The market, our clients and our competitors all force change on us.

7.4.3 What do we need to be sure of?

Before we grow our businesses, we need to be sure of a number of issues. Growth will require our resources and energy. It is important therefore to check that we are changing for positive reasons and that we have a sound base to expand from. Too many people think that expansion will be exciting. As a result, they spend a lot of time and money chasing rainbows rather than making sure their existing business is solid and secure. Expansion can be risky, as it will require a stronger and deeper resource base as well as a different set of skills. We need to minimise the risk by being clear about what we want to achieve and how we plan to go about it. We should talk other people to find out how they have expanded and what lessons they have learned.

Expansion may therefore involve new services and new ways of operating. It will certainly involve new relationships. We will need to develop trust with each other and quickly if the venture is to be a success. Geography always causes problems of communications, even where people know each other. This new structure requires us to develop and sustain trust quickly. It is important therefore to choose partners who share our values. Most importantly we will need to develop relationships with new people who we will trust with our image and reputation. We will need to be sure that our current business is not damaged. We have seen a number of UK companies going into joint ventures with North America, which did not work out well. UK confidence in them was damaged by what appeared to be naiveté on their part.

To expand our horizons, there are a number of key attributes we need to have, which include a need to:

1. be positive about ourselves, know what we excel at and more importantly what we enjoy doing,
2. work from a secure resource base and be clear about what we want to achieve,
3. be passionate about what we do and want to do so, that people will

          remember us as someone who inspires them to develop a relationship,

4.   follow what we enjoy, for example, if we like speaking other languages, then we should look for expansions which allows us to do more of that,

5.   be constantly on the look out for opportunities,

6.   listen to our clients to find out what they will want from us in the future,

7.   look for obvious synergies between professions, services and/or clients,

8.   look for 'matches' with other people as it is even more essential to work with people we trust when we have a geographical issue,

9.   talk to as many people as possible to find out what they have tried, what worked and why, what did not work and why, and

10.   be always willing to listen and learn.

The choice to expand or not is ours to take. Whether we take it or not depends on our individual aspirations. We can also decide whether to expand quickly or more slowly. We can also choose to downsize or become more specialised or niche.

7.5   Stage 3 Selection and implementation

We now need to make the correct choice for our firm from the four basic options available. Our choice will depend on our values, resources, market conditions, management skills and services. Each option has both positives and negatives associated with it, and demands distinct responses from our operational and strategic management.

In the sections below, each of the elements described above is highlighted in bold with an overall summary contained in the Options Selection Table at the end of this Chapter. This will allow us to check our own preferences against each option, thereby making our final selection easier.

7.5.1 Organic growth

Most firms adopt a strategy of organic growth without consciously thinking about it. Year on year, they try to increase profitability, gradually growing the resource, skill and client base. Those with key **values** of loyalty, independence, learning and a family orientation will be well suited to such a strategy. People who value excitement and change may well find it too limiting for them.

The **positives** of this option include that it:

- maintains control of the firm internally,
- works with our existing resource and skill base,
- works incrementally, allowing people to be comfortable with slow and steady change,
- ensures that we know the people we work with,
- allows clients to feel and experience continuity, and
- minimises disruption to work practices.

The **negatives** include that:

- it can be too slow to allow us to respond to market changes,
- people can become too comfortable and resistant to change,
- our clients may see us as old fashioned and stuck in our ways,
- younger professionals may see it as dull and unexciting,
- career advancement opportunities may be limited, restricted to 'dead man's shoes', and
- our resource and skill base may become too small or narrowly focused.

Our **management skills** need to focus on good resource management, maximising cash flow, and developing quality clients who are prepared to pay a fair fee and want to work with us long term. We need to have the ability to recruit potentially good people early in their career, allow them to learn and support them in their development through the firm. As a result, we need to be good at delegating and motivation, developing in-house training and career progression. We should be able to offer secondment for a short period to encourage them to identify other ways of working and expand their own network. People should feel supported, encouraged to learn and take on more responsibility.

Our growth is likely to be self-financing, building from the **resource** base that we have. Our services will be well established and across a wide sector and client base. We must be able to maintain and be known for the quality of our work. We must maximise cross selling to existing clients and attract new clients through our reputation. Client will experience continuity of **service** and personnel and will rely on us for a range of advice, seeing us as their first point of call when they need help. As a result, they will refer work to us and recommend us to their colleagues. This strategy works well in a **market** offering steady growth with clients seeking incremental changes in the range of services and delivery methods.

Our **Strategy Group** must concentrate on identifying and implementing ways of improving career development and progression, maximising cross selling and continuing to improve quality, our range of services and client loyalty.

7.5.2　Accelerated growth

I make no attempt to differentiate in this section between accelerated growth by way of merger, amalgamation, joint venture or some kind of looser association. In my opinion, they require the same values and skills. Some trading structures will involve more formal control over our resources, others less so. Regardless of structure, if we decide on a strategy of accelerated growth, our **values** must include sharing and being comfortable with change, uncertainty and flexibility as all of these will be tested over the short and medium term. To make the whole exercise worthwhile, we need to focus on profitability in the long term. We may set ourselves targets for an increase in fee turnover, but they must be matched with an increase in profitability.

The **positives** of an accelerated growth strategy include that it:

- is quicker than organic growth,
- brings in new people with skills, knowledge, fresh ideas and energy,
- brings additional resources,
- brings additional clients,
- may expand our geographical spread,
- must expand our range and depth of service, and
- increases the potential for improving quality, cross selling and profit margins.

The **negatives** include:

- a loss of independence and control,
- potential morale issues and uncertainty with staff,
- potential loss of personal touch with clients and partners,
- clients feeling unsure,

- problems with internal and external communications,
- problems with integrating technologies, systems and procedures, and
- increased management time before, during and after.

One of its key priorities is therefore developing the **management skills** required to manage this larger and unknown firm that has been created. We need to be good at networking to identify and check out new partners. We need to focus on communicating effectively, and identifying the potential for delegation and economies of scale. We need to get to grips with our expanded **resource** base quickly and get to know new people and identify their potential. We need to be able to convince people to stick with the pain of the change process for the long term. For example, short-term borrowings may be needed until the new firm settles down and client work regains momentum. As time and energy is absorbed dealing with the launch of the new entity, people will inevitably feel stretched. At the very time when clients need to be reassured about our attention to them, we may find ourselves stuck in internal merger meetings or even, physical moves of staff and/or offices.

This strategy will pay dividends if existing **clients** see value in the new shape. As a result, they must see an improvement from their perspective, for example, from the increased range or spread of services. We may be able to attract potentially *'better'* clients as we may be seen as a *'bigger player'* in the market. However, we must be careful to look after our existing clients and not take them for granted. There is a real risk that they see the personal touch and service levels dropping and fee levels increasing as people struggle to integrate previous work practices with the new order. Clients, like most people, are uncomfortable with change. They do not like to be taken for granted and will expect to be persuaded to remain with the new firm. Continuity of personnel is very important to them as they will have chosen to work with our previous firm for that reason i.e. they liked us and will not want to lose the personal connection they used to have.

This strategy works well if both firms have a good **resource** base and credit record sufficient to source additional borrowings in the short term. It works well in a buoyant and busy **market**, where people can see the potential that exists for attracting new business to be serviced from the combined resource and skill base. It may also increase our ability to attract quality staff as we will be seen as an ambitious and growing organisation. This increased base also offers the potential to develop new products and **services**, possibly through developing bespoke IT. It may also extend our geographical and sector reach, thereby reducing our exposure to changes in the market. This is where the true value of accelerated growth lies – in its potential to grow the firm exponentially by increasing the stability of the resource base, and attracting quality people and clients. One plus one must not simply make two but have the potential to become four. It must result in *more* than the same service to new clients and new services to existing clients. It must become new services to new clients. Our **Strategy Group** need to concentrate their innovation and energy on identifying and implementing ways of achieving that. They also need to be on the lookout for future potential merger, amalgamation and joint venture partners.

7.5.3 Downsize

The third option to be considered is that of downsizing. Sometimes this option is forced upon us by circumstances outwith our control such as the death or illness of a key person in our firm. This chance act requires us to look at our strategic options. Do we look for a new partner or another firm to join up with, or do we accept our new size and change our client base and workload accordingly? I know of several small firms who have adopted this strategy very successfully. They have either actively got rid of partners who were not pulling their weight, clients who were not valuable and/or focused on core work with improved margins and increased profitability.

Sometimes, we simply choose not to grow. As I mentioned at the outset, it is quite possible to be financially successful at a smaller size. Overheads will be less, staff worries reduced with the firm simply more manageable. Our **core values** will reflect this need to work with a small group of people, and/or actively seek an improved work and life balance.

The **positives** of downsizing include that:

- running costs will be reduced,
- our staff dependency is reduced,
- management time is reduced,
- internal communications will be easier,
- decisions are made more quickly, and
- we should to able to be more flexible and responsive.

The **negatives** include that:

- our current and future resources are more limited,
- our skill base may be insufficient to service client demands,
- head count may be stretched to cover workloads, holidays etc,
- we may not have resources to support changes in IT etc,
- internal morale may be affected by size reduction,
- clients may see the change in a negative way, and
- we may be not able to respond to future market changes.

Our **management skills** will need to concentrate on working out what and who is profitable and what and who is not. We may have to manage the exit of some people without damaging the morale of the remaining personnel and clients. As a result, we will need to focus our energy and skills on retaining key people. Our overheads should be reduced with our **resources** although limited, will be working more efficiently. Our range of **services** will be narrower and focused on the key clients we want to retain. This strategy works well in a constant **market**, where we can see continuity and dependability of client work, which will demand little change on the type of work we do or the way we deliver it. Our **Strategy Group** will be able to concentrate on identifying and implementing ways to make our limited resources work better for us.

7.5.4 Niche

One further option is that of becoming a niche or *'boutique'* firm. This implies that we focus firmly on one area of client service, sector of clients or area of specialism. For instance, we may decide to be media specialists, only work with retail clients or concentrate solely on commercial property work. Given the issues associated with trading as a partnership, it may make sense to limit the size of the firm in this way as it allows us to work with smaller groups of people and clients with less demand on our resources.

The **values** for such a firm will include expertise, high quality and recognition. This implies that the people attracted to working in such a firm will tend to be strong individuals who like the excitement of challenging and stretching work. As a result, they may not be the most manageable of professionals, preferring to work on their own and reluctant to follow procedures. The loss of key personnel and clients may cause considerable damage very quickly. Partnership, as we have discussed before, is a fragile animal, which is dependent on the commitment and confidence of the people working in it.

Resources in a niche firm can be tightly managed and focussed on proving a high quality expert service. We will be able to clearly identify the skills and types of people we want to attract and develop. These people may be expensive but profit margins for this type of work will be higher. There is a risk with a narrowly focused client base or service sector, that the level of work will fluctuate. For example, corporate activity and residential property can be very busy or very quiet. It is vital to use our resources efficiently and not panic into taking on work that is not cost effective. If at all possible, a niche practice should concentrate on work for which there is a constant or underprovided **market** demand for its type of expertise. The firm should strive to gain a reputation for being the **service** leaders in this field of work. It is also much easier to target new clients and referrals with a niche branding as we can place articles in specialist publications, speak at particular conferences and become a known and recognised name.

The **positives** include that it:

- allows us to control the type of work we agree to take on,
- attracts people who want to develop as specialists and experts,
- develops stronger ties with existing clients,
- allows us to target potential new clients and referrals more specifically,
- quickly develops a reputation for the firm,
- makes quality control and risk management easier to achieve,
- allows us to work with a smaller group of people,
- requires less overheads and resources in general,
- requires less management time due to reduced resources and more focussed client service delivery and marketing,
- is easier to establish our brand position and unique selling points, and
- should increase the quality of our work and profit margins

The **negatives** include that:

- we are more dependent on shifts in the market and legislation which could destroy our niche work base,
- we are more dependent on key clients due to smaller client base and

narrower service base,
- clients requiring other services that those we provide may go elsewhere,
- it makes us very dependent on a core of high quality people,
- too many 'experts' in a small firm may be difficult to manage,
- it may be difficult to maintain overall expertise, as people may become too narrowly focused in one field,
- career paths for younger professionals will be more limited due to smaller size,
- we may train professionals who leave and join our competitors, and
- it increases the risk to profitability and long-term success associated
- with key people leaving and taking important clients with them.

The key **management** skills of such a practice relate to addressing these negatives. We must be excellent at analysing and spotting market changes, maintain high quality control and good at marketing our brand. In addition, we must be able to turn away work which we are either not equipped to do or which will use up precious resources of people and time. This is a critical skill that is often overlooked and must be ruthlessly imposed. The managing partner of one extremely successful niche architect practice told me that he threw in the wastepaper bin any tender proposals which came in *without* letting his other partners see them as they would simply distract attention and waste time.

We must also have excellent people management skills and a great deal of patience. With our strong market positioning, we will be able to attract the best people in our field. We have to be able to retain them as the loss of key people will quickly damage our reputation. Therefore, we must be skilled at being aware of any unhappiness amongst essential personnel or clients, spend time with them to find out any concerns or worries. If there are issues of quality or service delivery, these must be addressed quickly and clients reassured. If internal people are unhappy, the source of the problem needs to be identified, dealt with and longer-term commitment demonstrated (see Chapters 4 and 8 on career planning). It is preferable to second a young professional out for a short while rather than risk losing him or her to a direct competitor.

The **Strategy Group** for such a firm must concentrate on market analysis watching out for signs of changes which are likely to impact on the demand for these niche services or the expertise required. We need to know as early as possible if there will be new legislation that directly affects us or our clients, if direct or indirect competition will encroach on our area or if a market downturn is anticipated. Dependent on such a small sector or client base, we have no other source of income. Operational issues such as maximising our branding and opportunities to attract and develop expertise should be the remit of the management of the firm.

7.6 Market positioning

Once the option has been selected and we have agreed how to implement it, we also need to consider how we position ourselves in the marketplace. It is important to be consistent with the message we give out and reinforce it with our clients. For example, if we decide that we are to be the market leaders in a particular field, then we need to speak at key conferences, be seen to be there as 'experts' and not sitting in the audience listening to other people speak. Similarly, if we position ourselves as being the approachable local professionals, then our offices in our main locations should look friendly, be accessible and easy to walk into.

It is equally important to reinforce this message with our staff. Too often I work with senior managers and partners who tell me how important they are in their marketplace and where they see themselves against other key players. However, when I run in-house client relationship training, their professional staff tell me that they feel they are merely second tier people trying to deliver the false promises made by their partners. If our staff do not believe they can deliver leading edge professional service, then our clients will also not be convinced. As a result, we need to spend time listening to staff to find out where *they* see the firm positioned, where the gaps are against what is being promised and agree how we can correct current problems with quality of service. At the same time, staff need to become more confident of their own abilities and the firm's abilities to deliver. It is possible to *'punch above our weight'* if we are focused, fit and trained.

Image, brand and reputation are the essence of a professional service firm. As we saw with the demise of Andersons, they go hand in hand with client confidence, partner and staff commitment, and current and future business success. Quality clients attract quality people and vice versa. This circle of success, once broken, becomes a vicious downward spiral of clients moving to other firms and staff and partners jumping ship. This gains momentum, so that, after only a few months, the firm is spiralling out of our control. The fragility of partnership, in particular, must never be underestimated. We can all think of firms in recent years that have atrophied and died.

We must pay attention and value our image, brand and reputation. In many cases, this will be judged by our existing people. Professionals work in tight networks of interconnections. We *'know'* what we think of people and their reputation through where they have trained, who they worked with in the past and how they behave when we work with them. We therefore judge other firms in the same way. If we see someone joining a firm, we will remark on whether they will *'fit in there'*. If we see someone we consider to be a *'good professional'* leaving another firm, we may read into that departure that there is some underlying problem with that firm. Much of our image is therefore subjective and determined by the way *other* people see us. It is not easy to build a brand in a service. Where a tangible product exists, we can offer 'free samples' and we can, with proper quality controls, replicate it time after time and in different geographical locations. Where we offer an intangible service, we are dependent on our clients' and other professionals' perception of us. Clients, in particular, continue to find it difficult to distinguish us from our competitors other than by what our people do, say and how they behave.

Our reputation is the key to our image and branding. It is also the key to attracting and keeping good people, and good clients. Our commercial and professional successes are intertwined.

7.7 Knowledge Management – knowing what we are good at

One final thought in relation to our strategic options is to consider how good we are at Knowledge Management. We looked at the growth in Knowledge Management as a strategic issue in Chapter 3. In my view, professional service firms have always been knowledge managers, delivering a service based on their knowledge and skills. This implies that we are good at managing the knowledge of our people and our firms, yet for many of us historically this was not the case. Anyone who has been given the task of developing 'firm styles', of introducing quality manuals and procedures know that professionals prefer to use their own documents or templates for letters, tenders or proposals. When I joined one firm, I was passed a large pile of proposed styles, which were quite literally covered in dust.

Regardless of which strategic option we choose, we *must* be good at knowledge management. Clients do not want to pay us by the hour to carefully craft reams of paperwork. Given current client demands and workloads, we do not have the time or the energy to start every project with a blank sheet of paper. Regulatory and risk management compliance require that we follow accepted templates and procedures. If we are a niche firm, our expertise is based on our ability to harness and grow our knowledge management. If we growing organically, we need to be able to develop our young professionals and train them in our way of working and thinking. If we are merging with another firm or entering into a joint venture, we need to be able to encapsulate and share our knowledge in such a way that we can maximise the advantages that our combined knowledge will bring.

The essential element in knowledge management is that people share information. We will look at how to achieve this in more detail in the next Chapter.

Conclusions

Choosing the right development option for our firms does not happen by chance. It requires up to date knowledge of the market and careful identification of the choices available. We must match any selection with the core values of our firm, as well as what we want to achieve for it in the long term.

To implement our choice, we must think innovatively and identify key people to drive it through within specified timescales. Each strategic option brings with it core skills, resources, positives and weaknesses. We must be consistent in our choice and reinforce the same message in our marketing, brand, image and reputation. However, it is also important to remain flexible and receptive to changes in the market and/or client demands.

Key Action Points
1.   be clear from the outset about what we want to achieve
2.   make sure that our choice reflects our core values

3.   apply our market analysis to our individual situation
4.   listen to our clients and what they tell us about future demands
5.   think long term about the need to expand
6.   support our choice with key skills and resources
7.   ensure that we send a consistent message to the marketplace
8.   pay attention to our Knowledge Management

Table 7.5 Options Selection Table

	Values	Resources	Market	Management skills	Services	Positives	Negatives	Strategy Group
Organic growth	Loyalty Independence Family approach Learning	Existing	Steady growth and change in demand and type	Resource maximisation Coaching Motivation Good recruitment and retention	Established Quality Wide based Cross selling	Control Know people Continuity	Slow Too comfortable Seen as unexciting	Improving career progression, quality, range of services, client loyalty
Accelerated growth	Sharing Change Flexibility	Expanded short-term borrowings Longer-term economies of scale	Buoyant Rapid changes in type of work and method of delivery	Networking Communications Excellent resource management Delegation	Wider based than before, both in geography and range	Fast New skills and resources More clients and depth	Loss of control Lack of knowledge of new resource base Communications and integration challenges	Developing new partners, new services and new clients
Downsize	Working alone Work/life balance	Cost efficiency	Constant Little change in demand or type of service	Resource management Managing exits	Narrower	More manageable	Effect on morale and future resource base	Improving resource efficiency
Niche	Expertise High quality Recognition	Existing Potential for higher margin profits	Constant or undersupplied demand for expertise	Quality control Ability to say no Market awareness Branding	Leaders in field	Controllable Build and maintain reputation more easily	Susceptible to market changes Dependency on key people and clients	Market analysis and forecasting

8
SHAPING UP FOR SUCCESS

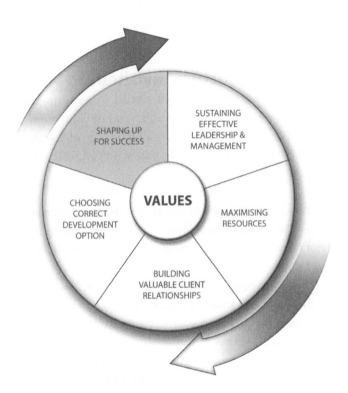

8.1 Introduction

Throughout this book, I have emphasised the importance of being able to change. By working our way through the Model for Success, we convince people of the *benefits* of change and as a result, develop a *willingness* to change. In Chapter 2, we looked at the importance of matching our operational structure and shape to support the direction we are taking. I deliberately used both words 'shape' and 'structure' to emphasise that organisational structure by itself is not enough.

Many organisations think that producing an organisational chart will somehow define how people will behave and how the business will operate. Structure by itself simply lays down a template of what should happen. However, we need to define the shape as well – i.e. how people communicate and behave, what skills they need and how we want them to 'grow'. Overall, our intention in relation to securing the correct shape and structure for our firm, is to build our resource base. This includes our internal skills, knowledge and expertise as well as our external contacts and reputation. In this Chapter, we will look at ways of sustaining flexibility, managing mobility and tackling succession planning.

8.2   The correct structure revisited

I mentioned in Chapter 2 that I did not intend to recommend one trading structure over another. Each of us has our own set of values and our structure must reflect these. For example, if we have a high value of learning and loyalty, our structure will be supportive and collegiate with people sharing knowledge, skills and clients.

Particularly with partnerships, there are almost as many alternative structures as there are firms. The rules of some professional bodies still limit sharing profits with people not members of that particular body. As a result, some firms:

- have a few equity partners who control the firm,
- have both equity and salaried partners,
- have partners working their way to parity through passage of time,
- share profits based on peer voting,
- have senior managers who share in the profits to some extent,
- adopt an *'eat what you kill'* approach to profit shares,
- operate as if they trade as companies or franchises, and/or
- have set up different trading entities for different services.

Some operate a combination of these or have developed unique shapes of their own. In my experience, each one brings its own advantages and disadvantages and all have to be managed successfully. To start to achieve that, we must be clear about what structure we currently are operating. As outlined in Chapter 2, we need to map out our organisational structure and check it against the reality of what is actually happening. It is equally important to capture our external 'shape', including who refers work to us, what work we refer out and how easily we can source external advice and support. A growing number of professional firms seem to have forgotten that they need to build this external resource base, taking a very short-term view of what help and support they provide to other players in the market.

From the outset, I have argued that managing professionals is not easy and cannot be achieved by slavishly following HR tools such as written job descriptions or appraisals. Indeed, such formality can inhibit our ability to work persuasively and effectively for our clients. How do we manage our professionals in such a way as to allow them flexibility and allow us some measure of control and consistency?

One way to achieve this is to have a clear, defined and objective career structure. This can supplemented by using mentors, coaches and client feedback to reinforce what aspects of individual work that our clients value. As always, it is important to focus on both the good and weaker aspects of people's work practices.

I know of a number of firms who employ full time Human Resource managers and departments, and others who take the opposite view, preferring to include formal people management in line managers' operational duties. HR specialists are professionals in their own fields and can add considerable value. Similarly, if the partners do not value their expertise, they will be unable to contribute positively to the firm's future success. As always, it is essential to choose whichever solution matches the resources and values of our individual firms. It is also important to remember that professionals are not easy to manage and must be tackled in an advanced way. Our review of Emotional Intelligence and Knowledge Management in Chapter 3 provides us with some help about how to achieve that.

8.2.1 Emotional Intelligence and its effect on our shape

We have already considered the growing importance of emotional intelligence as an acceptable part of business management. It is argued that we cannot divorce our emotions from our success at work. We have talked about the importance of managing the emotional issues of behaviour and conflict. We also looked at mistakes and their impact on our performance in Chapter 5 in risk management. Similarly fatigue plays a big part in the quality of our judgement and the advice we provide. It is generally accepted that intuition plays a large part in our decision-making process, especially for senior managers. Good leaders are now described within an emotional framework, such as the ability to inspire trust and motivate people. Good professionals *care* about what they do and our clients want us to *care* about them. All of this influences the shape of our organisations i.e. the way that people interact with each other.

It is important to accept the part that emotions play in our professional and business environment. Partnerships are particularly prone to emotional dynamics as they are so much based around relationships, values and trust. Any type of partnering (social and business) involves emotions. As we discussed in Chapter 7, where our values and cultures differ from our prospective partners, it is better to walk away.

Some emotions are to be encouraged such as caring, passion and commitment. We need to be confident, sure of our own abilities (when such assurance is merited), able to stand our ground and protect our client's best interest. We need to have integrity, be assertive and self-aware. Others emotions, such as arrogance, selfishness and intolerance need to be discouraged. In my experience, it is a very narrow line between self-assurance and arrogance. Quite often that line is crossed through stress and tiredness, both of which cause other emotions such as feeling overwhelmed with workloads or time pressures, a fear of not knowing or of making mistakes. We cannot control people or their emotions, but it is our job as senior managers to identify these triggers and minimise their effect. Most people do not like behaving badly and realise when they are doing it. They can be helped. However, the minority who like to behave badly should be removed from our structure as they do considerable damage to our shape. They create a sea of emotions ranging from active dislike to fear and resentment and tire out and exhaust other people.

8.2.2 Knowledge Management and its effect on our structure

We have looked at the importance of knowledge management for professional service firms in some detail. Its impact on our shape and structure was significant even before 'Knowledge Management' became officially recognised. Similarly, the layout of our organisations, the geography of different departments and floors has an effect on how well knowledge is shared and pooled.

Historically, the professions passed on knowledge from senior practitioner to junior, with people becoming recognised as experts in key subject areas through years of experience and practice. Nowadays, technology allows us to capture some of that implicit knowledge in a tangible form, such as the development of styles, pro-forma documents and reports. Sector and client knowledge can be pooled into databases, accessible to people in different geographical locations. Client checklists can allow us to routinise the application of our knowledge, ensuring that everyone can adopt *'best practice'*.

However, knowledge management is not about IT alone. Office layout and culture are equally important. People have to be willing to share their knowledge and expertise. I can think of one large public sector organisation that invested hundreds of senior management hours into developing their Knowledge Management systems, which failed because their culture was one that rewarded people for individual performance, with the result that they refused to share their knowledge.

It is therefore important to recognise and reward 'knowledge people' as defined in Chapter 3. These are people who share information, see links and build bridges both internally and externally, who are enthusiastic and energetic. Many firms now accept this, focusing on recruiting and retaining professionals who fit this profile. We must also look at ways of developing these abilities and of encouraging people to share and help each other.

8.3   Flexibility and the ability to change

Whatever structure and shape we choose, we have to build flexibility into it. It is not possible to develop an organisational chart, introduce written job descriptions and stick to them slavishly. Quite apart from coping with people on holiday, ill or leaving, no professional can say with certainty what he or she will be expected to do to complete a job for a client. Each client is different. Each project is different. Few of us would want to be so constrained, as the pleasure we get out of working with clients often derives from our ability to interpret our knowledge and skills and apply it to that particular client or situation. Additionally, as we have discussed in Chapter 5, clients want that interpretation and our competitive advantage lies in our ability give it.

We also need the ability to change – to grow and develop as professionals. Few of us have pursued a straight career path to where we are now. We may have entered our profession with a desire to do one type of work and were offered the opportunity to work with a particular client or particular job which resulted in a change of direction or a growing interest and expertise in another area. We may have seen market or regulatory changes that resulted in a new field developing when we were in the right place to take advantage of that. We may have enjoyed working with one client so much that we moved to join them. We may have had the opposite experience, being forced to change direction as a result of fluctuations in client and/or workload demands. Our technical knowledge base cannot and does not stand still.

In addition, we have a professional responsibility to bring on and develop younger professionals. We need to become teachers, delegating work so that younger people can learn and improve their own knowledge and skills. As a result, we ourselves need to learn new skills and ways of working, to focus our time and energy in different ways. We all need the ability to change, regardless of how senior we are in our organisations.

People provide us with our current competitive advantage. We need to attract and retain quality people and clients, as each feed off the other. We need to motivate people to use their knowledge and expertise to provide exceptional services. We need to allow them to hoard their energy and time for direct client contact, difficult work and using their ingenuity to come up with innovative solutions to client problems. We need to ensure that the shape and skills we have matches our strategy for the future. All of this will allow us to sustain our future competitive advantage.

8.3.1 Reward people

As a result, it is important to recognise and reward this willingness to change. There are two elements to this – the first is to define 'good behaviour' and the second is to work out a reward mechanism.

Good behaviour must include:

1.   behaving in a way that reflects the firm's values,
2.   taking responsibility for themselves and their work,

3. sharing or cross referring clients,
4. referring work to external contacts or partners,
5. developing and/or mentoring more junior people,
6. helping young professionals with their professional body exams, work experience or entry requirements,
7. offering to take on a key project or work on the Strategy Group,
8. contributing to the image or brand of the firm by specific activities, such as writing articles, speaking at conferences, charity events,
9. developing a new area of expertise, establishing a new department or service, and/or
10. introducing new procedures, ways of working, knowledge management.

The opposite of type of behaviour should be discouraged. This includes refusing to pass on work outwith one's area of experience, being abusive or unhelpful to junior people, and failing to follow established procedures and/or introduce new ways of working.

These criteria also provide a list of what we need to measure when it comes to rewarding people. As a result, our systems must be able to capture:

1. internal referral work and its sources,
2. external referrals and introductions received back,
3. time spent working with more junior people and details of what has been achieved,
4. feedback (formal and informal) from junior staff about what they have gained from support from more senior people,
5. key project / Strategy Group accomplishments,
6. details of articles, speaking appearances, etc and feedback from these,
7. increases in expertise and skills of the firm, and
8. improvements in work practices, cost savings and the like.

Our reward mechanism should be as objective as possible. It is essential to devise some tangible way of demonstrating that *'good behaviour'* has been recognised and not taken for granted. This can include reporting on these activities monthly, through formal time recording codes, personal or business development logs and/or captured in our Knowledge Management systems, with values and ratings applied to them. The formality of the Continuing Professional Development requirements of our professional bodies can be used to collate a lot of this type of information. People should be recognised for their commitment to this and not just for the client fees they generate.

It is important to look at our share of profits or reward structure as these must also reward good behaviour. This is always one area where the professionals show their innovative skills. In my experience, there appears to be no limit to the possible options when it comes to working out partners' share of profits, ranging from firms where all partners closet themselves away every year for a day and thrash out individual profit share through to firms where one partner makes the decision on his or her own. I cannot provide examples of what is a 'good profit share structure' and what is not.

What works for one firm will not work for others. As with other areas discussed, whatever structure is chosen must work for *that* firm and reflect its values. If, for example, the firm places considerable emphasis on teamwork, then the split of profits should reflect that. If the firm wants to 'grow' their own future partners, then the partners who are prepared to send time and energy coaching and mentoring others should be rewarded for that. Most reward structures will contain some element of subjective judgement with the result that the people who make that judgement must have the trust and respect of other people.

8.3.2   Instil energy and innovation

Whatever shape or structure we adopt must instil energy in everyone. I have worked with a number of organisations whose structures have resulted in endless meetings and email communications. Their organisational structure demands consultation with every head of department and their shape lacks the skill base to achieve major change. Everyone seems to have to meet to debate every issue and little ever happens. A trawl of the formal minutes of such meetings often discloses that it takes a minimum of 18 months between an idea being mooted and a decision being made. In such circumstances, implementation only happens when one person *drives* the idea through, exhausting him or herself and others in the process.

It is important to have a structure and shape that *allows* things to happen, where people are given the responsibility to do rather than talk about doing. By creating the ability to change, the Model for Success allows the development of the shape and skills, such as decision making, sharing and learning, needed to support implementation.

Another essential aspect of our structure and shape is its ability to instil innovation. People must be allowed to learn, to see if we can do things differently and to suggest changes to the way we work, the clients we work with, and/or the services we provide.

In Chapter 3 we looked at the increasing importance of innovation in our ultimate competitive advantage. When people show initiative and suggest improvements, this should be recognised and encouraged. If, for example, a younger professional offers to join the Strategy Group, our shape should be able to accommodate that. If a junior person wants to become involved in winning new clients or visiting existing ones to see how they conduct their business, then that should be possible. We should also encourage secondment or working with other types of professionals, as in my experience, it is amazing how little real contact there is between the professions. For example, the medical profession have developed some excellent personal development models involving peer review and self-reflection that some construction and property professionals could learn a lot from.

Another useful project is to ask junior professionals to gather stories about our organisations. One module of client relationship training I have developed asks people to bring to the session three stories telling how the firm provided exceptional service to its clients. I am often disappointed about how few stories seem to be available, especially as senior people involved have been telling me how exceptional the firm is in its field! Once identified, these stories can then be told and retold with pride. Young professionals in particular, benefit from being able to recount stories as it helps them develop confidence to speak to clients, certain in the knowledge that they have something to be proud of and say about the firm.

8.4   Mobility in the market

Every week we see examples of equity partners, senior people and even whole departments and teams of people moving between firms. In my opinion, this is one of the most significant new trends for managers of professional firms as until recently, it was deemed to be professionally unacceptable to move firms too often. It seemed to imply that the individual concerned was in some way *'unstable'* or professionally suspect.

This trend is significant because such movement has the potential to have a major destabilising effect on professional firms. Professional service firms and partnerships in particular are inherently unstable as they are made up of key individuals who clients see represent the 'persona' of the firm. Once they leave, firms can atrophy and wither away. Good people, seeing little point in continuing with a *'dying'* firm, seek new positions with the result that the death of the firm comes quicker.

This results in a number of competing demands on our management skills. How can we harness this current mobility in the marketplace to achieve positive results for our firms? For example, how can we introduce innovation, tailored services and develop long-term relationships with key clients when staff keep changing? How can we build trust and collaboration when people leaving push the culture of the firm the other way? In my view, the answers lie in analysing why this is happening, and the effect it has.

8.4.1 Why is this happening?

There are a number of general reasons for increasing mobility. We have considered before that the 'carrot' of partnership is no longer enough to persuade young professionals to commit to one firm early on their career. Most want to build their CVs by working with a range of firms and clients. Individual career development has therefore become a stronger driver than loyalty to one firm. The increasing numbers of women entering the professions inevitably means more career interruptions of whatever length and in whatever form individuals may decide.

Both these trends have to be accepted and worked into the operational management of the firm. Young professionals of both sexes are an essential part of the future of the professions. It is still important to train them well and build them into our professional network. If they decide to move to obtain more experience, they will remain colleagues we may have to work with in the future. Our professional network is tight, with the result that it is important to build relationships rather than create bad feeling and resentment towards the firm or the individual. Career interruptions should be treated in the same way. I worked part time for some of my legal professional life and my clients, happy to trust me to get the job done, never objected in any way.

More significant, is the growing trend of partners, senior managers, associates and even complete teams moving between direct competitors. (Indeed it can be argued that people should never be taken for granted and that good people must be persuaded *not* to leave all the time.) This trend has serious implications for both the internal management of the firm and its external image.

There can be both personal and business reasons behind this type of movement. From a personal point of view, an individual may choose to leave as the result of:

- feeling undervalued or taken advantage of,
- frustrations about the way the firm is being managed,
- his or her professional values being put under pressure or not respected,
- a colleague being treated badly,
- partnership issues not being addressed and allowed to fester,
- lack of forward progress and implementation of change,
- a climate of conflict and 'fiefdoms',
- poor quality of work and clients,
- feeling of not doing a worthwhile job, and/or
- no clear career route to progress through the firm.

As a result, people will move to resolve these issues. For example, moving to another firm may offer the 'carrot' of short-term higher quality work and/or an opportunity to make partner.

From the business point of view, asking certain individuals to leave may result from:

- a downturn in overall fee income,
- a reduction in profits,
- a shift in the profitability of some areas of client work,
- increasing competition in the marketplace,
- pressure to take short-term decisions, and/or
- the need to reposition the firm.

In most cases personal and business issues are inter-related, as the tensions and strains of one feed into the other. When one partner is unhappy, he or she will often talk to other people within the firm. Particularly when the firm is experiencing cash flow problems, most people in the firm will be aware of these difficulties. Partnership is a fragile animal with people and their morale playing a large part in its internal operations as well as the quality of client service delivery. As a result, when key professionals leave a firm for whatever reason, their departure needs to be actively tackled, not ignored or dealt with in a hostile and volatile way. To adopt the latter approaches merely polarises an already difficult situation. People leaving the firm can create problems, but in my experience, it can also create opportunities.

8.4.2 The problems caused

The problems raised by people leaving the firm are well known to most professionals as most of us have experienced the stresses of working in a situation where senior people leave. Because of the personal nature of partnership, these resemble those involved in divorce! Some people see it as a personal betrayal and refuse to deal with the individuals concerned. Others blame the managing partner for what has happened. Others are terrified of the effect on the firm, run around 'protecting' their clients and their work, and others are jealous of those who are 'escaping' and whisper their negativity to anyone who will listen to them.

Generally speaking, the problems fall into two categories – practical and emotional. The practical problems should be governed by any partnership agreement and include managing:

- the financial aspects, including capital and cash flow implications,
- the hand over of work in progress,
- client transition, and
- junior staff and direct reports.

If there is no up to date partnership agreement, the options are more open to negotiation and will as a result, take much time and energy. Getting partners to make quick pragmatic decisions is difficult enough at the best of times, and in my experience, this is *not* one of those times! This highlights the importance of actively managing the emotional problems caused. It is amazing how much of 'old baggage' and personal vindictiveness will reappear as partners take other partners leaving so very personally!

In addition to the particular practical problems caused by the individual(s) leaving, there will be more general 'knock on' effect relating to trust and morale. People will start to raise questions around management issues, such as:

- How can we delegate when people may leave and take our clients and our knowledge with them?
- How can we build this business and invest in it for the long term when people keep leaving?
- How can we be expected to cross sell when there is no continuity?
- How can we achieve consistency of client service?
- How can we be expected to share knowledge and take time out from direct client work to train people?
- How can we achieve any kind of succession planning?
- How can we sort out quality and workload problems?
- How can we cope with all this fire fighting?

Personal questions revolve around relationships and trust:

- Who can I trust?
- How can I cope with losing a colleague and friend?
- How do I know that this will not happen again?
- Who can I ask for help and share my expertise with?
- What will be the effect on my support staff?
- Will I be expected to take on more work?
- What will be the effect on my earnings?
- What will be the effect on me?
- What will my clients think?

As we have often discussed, partnership implies trust, mutual support and sharing resources. Seeing people leaving challenges all of these.

8.4.3 What needs to be done

What needs to be done to stabilise the firm? First of all, we need to prioritise the amount of time and energy this will require from our managers and leaders.

This challenge has to be accepted by everyone as a key priority for the firm. Identifying the underlying issue is the second step. Exit interviews can be an excellent way to get people to talk off the record about the ultimate causes of their dissatisfaction but it is usually too late at that stage to prevent those people from leaving. It may also be too late to undo any knock-on effect and damage, both internally and externally.

As soon as someone announces their intention to leave, several definitive actions need to be taken. These include that:

1. the individuals concerned must be spoken with to find out why they are leaving and how they intend to behave in the intervening period,
2. if these are valuable people, we need to ascertain whether they can be persuaded to change their mind,
3. if they will not damage the firm by their exit, we need to agree a quick and positive process for them to leave with the minimum amount of disruption, cost and time,
4. we should agree with them both internal and external communication of this news and its timing,
4. we must continually reinforce the positive message that the firm is in control of the situation and when people cause disruption and negativity they are dealt with,
5. all information should be disseminated through face-to-face discussions with key people as this allows us to identify whether they are also feeling uncertain about their future with the firm, and if so, we are able to provide them with reassurance and,
5. key external clients and contacts must also be told directly about what is happening, again to reinforce the positive message and demonstrate that there will be no direct effect on the quality of their services.

The timing of all of this is crucial, which is why it must be given priority and resources. I continue to hear stories of firms insisting that partners, senior people and their teams work out six months' notice. In my opinion, the thought of having an individual or a group of people, regardless of how professionally they are behaving within the firm that length of time beggar's belief! For a full half of a trading year, the firm is forced to work every day with people who have decided to leave. Grasping the nettle and therefore paying people to leave is important. One accountant was bemoaning to me over lunch one day the lack of commercial reality that seems to grip professionals when faced with a partner leaving. He was acting for a law firm and had just left a particularly trying meeting with them. He described that emotions were running high with partners feeling betrayed and let down, rather than accepting the business tenor of the situation. His clients felt that they would prefer winding up the partnership with all its attendant damage to cash flow, clients and reputation rather than pay out the exiting partner what he was asking for as his share of work in progress. He was trying to persuade them that that would serve no-one well.

8.4.4 Opportunities created?

People leaving can seem like a management nightmare with a great deal of effort going in to effect damage limitation. However, in my experience, it is possible to see it instead as an opportunity to address a number of issues. These could include that:

1. tackling it in a positive way will demonstrate in a tangible way that the firm is capable of coping with change,
2. more often than not, the person leaving has been unhappy for some time affecting his or her attitude or behaviour and influencing those around them,
3. even where the person leaving is seen to be crucial or unique, his or her departure will provide the firm with the chance to review workloads and client relationships which perhaps were being taken for granted,
4. the more entrenched partners will as a result, be forced to change their ways of working to absorb adjusted workloads,
5. younger professionals will see and may indeed seize the chance to progress within the firm, and
6. the firm will be forced to review its structure, finances, operation and succession plans.

Many of these may be issues that the firm should have been addressing anyway. Indeed, its failure to deal with some of them may be the cause of people leaving.

Opportunities created for the firm include the chance to:

- recruit new energy and skills,

- develop new client and business connections,
- introduce new knowledge and expertise,
- enhance existing services, and
- develop existing people who may have become stale and stuck in their ways.

For individuals, changing firms offers the opportunities of a new challenge, the stretch of new work, clients, colleagues and ways of working. Bringing in new people should always be seen as an opportunity for everyone to learn and challenge old assumptions. New people will see things with fresh eyes and as a result, should be debriefed after their first couple of months to identify improvements to existing practices. They are much cheaper than paying external consultants to do the same internal review exercise.

8.4.5 How to prevent it happening

At indicated above, good people always have the choice to leave. They cannot be forced to stay or commit themselves to working with our firm in perpetuity. As a result, we need to create a culture of mutual support, where people feel valued and loyal.

We must therefore:

1. deliver our core values in some tangible way, for example, if we have a value of teamwork or mentoring, we should reward team successes or the achievement of individual achievements,
2. ensure that our performance remuneration encourages reciprocity and joint effort,
3. introduce and follow through on structured career planning, including progression from trainee through to partner with clear incremental steps,
4. do not allow people to feel that the firm has 'favourites',
5. review current workloads with people to reinforce that they are being provided with both short and long-term career development gains,
6. allow people to tackle a variety of work to enhance skills and expertise, which also develops their ability to learn, be flexible and cope with change,
7. provide regular constructive feedback and ongoing support through an effective appraisal process and by a coach or mentor,

8. address problems or frustrations as these will fester and infect other people, and

9. pay attention to '*distress flares*', because when people seem to be acting in a stressed way, it is usually because they are!

8.5   Shaping the skill base and sustaining success

Succession planning involves inherent contradictions. On the one hand, there is the need to make plans to generate certainty and on the other, people are individuals and cannot be replicated. The market and our clients constantly change and with it the demand for our services. The better we are at forward planning and anticipating these changes, the better we are at managing our shape and structure to respond. The current shortage of skilled construction workers illustrates how difficult it is to increase the skill base in the short term.

As a result, we need to shape our skill base to cope with such fluctuations and demands. People should be encouraged to take a wider rather than narrower approach to their personal development. As we have discussed before, formal role reviews and/or mentors should encourage this through a structured career progression.

Succession planning must be discussed openly and regularly with individual partners and senior managers. It is essential not to make assumptions about what they will want to be doing in the future. For instance, not everyone wants to work until they reach sixty or sixty five or continue to shoulder the workloads and responsibilities they had at forty, and not everyone wants to make a lot of money at every stage of their career. Effective management should mean that there will be no surprises! Succession planning must include replacement of technical and management expertise. The attrition rate for senior managers in HR, Finance and Marketing in particular, continues to be high with an average duration in these roles of about 2 years. Yet, 2 years is not long enough to measure the significant impact of many management projects, such as client development, integration of a merger or geographical expansion. It is unfair to rotate or sack senior managers simply because no positive impact on the bottom line is perceived within that time frame. Similarly 2 years is too long for partners to talk about tackling key projects without actually doing them. As a result, frustrations build as senior managers feel unappreciated and unsupported.

Partners still talk to me about the *'poisoned chalice'* of management as if it is something that has to be endured. Management has to be seen as an important element of professional and business success. It must be given as high a profile as high quality client work. For example, one firm known for its stability and consistency asks all of its partners every year to detail how they have *contributed* to the firm's management. Not surprising the culture of that firm is inclusive and supportive, with young professionals keen to join it and stay with it. External academic and formal qualifications can help to promote such a profile. Early integration of management skills into career profiles is also useful. The use of external experts also helps bring credibility and fresh energy.

To become a good partner, able to contribute to the current and future success of our firms, is neither an easy task nor one that happens by chance. We cannot assume that it will happen naturally or that people will intuitively know what is required of them. Younger professionals need to be shown the route to partnership and what will be required of them along that road. It is important to look at the composite attributes required to identify areas which require improvement within the firm or individually. Proper career development is essential with firms creating their own template of the skills and attributes required. Developing and keeping good people is fundamental to the current and future success of our firms.

8.5.1 What makes a good partner?

It is rare to find a formal job description for a partner within a professional firm, yet most professionals aspire to become one. It is usually assumed that everyone knows what makes a good partner, but it is harder to formally articulate its key attributes. Indeed, many professionals find it difficult to agree on a composite, constructive description of such a person, preferring to concentrate on providing me with examples of *'bad'* partners. However, it is vital to be able to specify the key elements of what would make a good partner.

We have already developed a number of profiles that help us do this. In Chapter 2, we looked at common core elements that included technical and professional skills, the ability to deliver high quality client services, good leadership and management skills, and a strong external network and reputation. In Chapter 3, we discussed the profile of a 'knowledgeable person' which included someone who shares information and communicates well, who likes helping other people, is energetic, inspires trust and builds relationships, is respected and technically skilled. Each firm needs to consider the elements important to it and as always reflects its core values.

This need to build a partner profile is important for the reasons we have discussed before. First of all, the market is becoming tighter, resulting in a need to plan ahead to achieve business continuity. Secondly, the partners of the firm set the image and tone of the firm, and as a result, influence the behaviour which other people in the firm adopt. And thirdly, with so much change in today's market, succession and career planning are becoming increasingly important for those of us seeking to retire from practice and for younger professionals aspiring to have a long-term future in our firms.

Following the five segments of the Model allows us to identify that a good partner is one who:

1.   displays leadership and management skills,
2.   makes effective use of resources
3.   has a strong client focus,
4.   thinks strategically about the firm, and
5.   adapts the shape and structure of his or her people.

Attribute 1 displays leadership and management skills

The key skills of leadership and management include the ability to inspire trust and respect. We trust people who share our values of professionalism and integrity. Good managers are consistent in their dealings with people, communicate effectively, openly and impartially. They deal with conflict proactively and set clear and impartial standards for people to work to. They accept that managing professionals is not easy and encourage people to agree and work *with* rather than obey them.

Attribute 2 makes effective use of resources

It is taken for granted nowadays that a good partner is technically skilled and competent. He or she will understand and apply good risk management to client work and staff supervision. In addition, he or she will be comfortable with generating and achieving time and fee targets.

However, a good partner needs to go beyond this and be able to use management information to make choices about how work is handled and by whom, to calculate the 'profitability' of types of client work and react accordingly by improving internal efficiency at the same time as maintaining the quality of the service provided.

Attribute 3 has a strong client focus

Most clients want a solution to their problem rather than be told about the process involved. It is important therefore to get to know clients and build their loyalty. A good partner is able to develop a relationship which is valuable to both sides – giving clients what they want, when and how *at the same time* as making a profit. The key skills of effective client management are listening, clear communications and delivering high quality, consistent service.

Attribute 4 thinks strategically about the firm

Many partners tell me they aspire to think high-level thoughts about the firm but simply never get the time or the energy to do it. Yet the most successful firms plan for and apply longer-term thinking. They know what they want to achieve, how they define success and how they will get there. Most professionals are trained to be risk adverse, yet strategic thinking requires creative thought. As a result, a good partner is able to balance risk with reward, thinking through practical problems related to change and growth and how to resolve them.

Whilst we accept that flexibility is essential in the current marketplace, we need to adopt an overall strategy and most importantly, implement it. For example, to adopt a niche strategy implies concentrating on certain specialisms and building skills and the reputation to support that. Pursuing a strategy of accelerated growth implies concentrating on achieving management expertise and high gearing of resources and people.

Attribute 5 adapts the shape and structure of his or her people

Thinking strategically implies more than simply talking about future plans. We have to be able to put these into practice. Flexibility and adaptability are essential. As a result, good partners are able to adapt the shape of their teams and the skills of their people. Given professionals' natural inclination to be independent and 'loners' this is not easy to achieve. In my experience, team working does not come naturally to most professionals unless they are in charge of the team!

As a result, partners must be rewarded for sharing clients and information, for spending time training others and allowing them to learn. Good partners are therefore able to use the trust and respect they have generated to encourage people to work together rather than in isolation.

If all of this seems a tall order, it is. A good partner cannot concentrate on only one attribute of the Model at the expense of the others. To do so creates tensions within the firm as other people end up doing more than their fair share of other aspects. For example, it is unfair to leave cash flow worries to other people when every partner has a responsibility to deliver high quality client work and make it profitable. Over and above all, we must put this list into the context of our own firm and its future aspirations. If for example, we want to be a niche practice, we must develop the expertise to support that. If we intend to use IT to handle large volumes of client work, we must have partners who are able to and comfortable with managing that.

Some people reading this book may well be aspiring to become a partner. Historically, making partner was seen as the pinnacle of professional life. More recently, being a partner is seen as being weighed down with the responsibilities of running a business in an extremely competitive and demanding marketplace.

This reinforces the need for proper career planning. The skills included in Attribute 1 (leadership and management), Attribute 4 (strategic thinking) and Attribute 5 (shape and structure adaptability) will not necessarily have been developed on the way to making partner, which traditionally will have concentrated on Attribute 3 (client service) and elements of Attribute 2 (resource management). Some people will naturally be better at some more than others. Some will need encouragement to develop a balanced range of skills. It is important to develop all of the attributes, by way of mentoring, coaching or targeted education and training. Making it to partner is not the end of the road in terms of career and skill development.

8.5.2 The selection process

Selecting people as partners can be divisive. Bringing in outsiders can disappoint and demotivate existing key personnel. Choosing one internal candidate over another will cause similar problems. If people try to seek preferential treatment by threatening to leave or asking for more money, then they should not be '*rewarded*' for behaving in this way. It is essential therefore to ensure that the selection process is:

1.   clearly defined and objective,
2.   transparent and applied with consistency, and
3.   rewards long-term commitment and contribution.

Succession planning should be discussed openly. As always, it is important to depersonalise these discussions. Partnership agreements, supported by business plans, should set the parameters for selection, maternity leave and retiral. People will then be clear about what they have signed up for. Deviating from these can cause dangerous precedents.

Choosing one person over another will always cause disappointment. It is important not to allow it to build into resentment. This is where having defined incremental stages moving towards partnership pays dividends. When people are clear about what is expected of them and what they need to achieve, they cannot argue that they have been treated unfairly. If they have been educated into the financial side of the firm, they will understand what the business needs to achieve by making them partner.

Professional partnerships operate unique structures. They are not like limited companies where management and ownership are separate. They have no automatic hierarchy of authority or decision making. They all operate, manage and function in their own way. The more sophisticated of them will have formalised management and partnership responsibilities but these are all predicated by the need for consensus and trust. Some will have developed career paths but even these will be based on subjectivity and other people's opinions and influence.

In addition, '*professional behaviour*' almost assumes an arrogance of attitude. It certainly implies an independence of thought to ensure that the needs of clients are preferred over and above all demands of management and budgets. Professionals are often judged on their '*force of personality*'. As we have discussed before, this can spill over into a 'closed shop' approach to valuing other professionals. Professionals judge the competence of each other through tight networks. This makes it very difficult for a new breed of people to be allowed in.

Many young professionals are questioning *'what's so great about making partner?'* as nowadays it appears to bring with it unlimited liability and increasingly demanding clients. A certain quality of life and level of income is no longer assured. Why should we take on this burden of responsibility and worry? Is it worth the return?

Most professionals do not make partners until their late 20s or early 30s. The route to equity partner often takes another five to ten years. Women have to make hard choices during that period unlike their male counterparts who can usually select both options. Many professional women opt to put off having children until they in their 40s. Others have opted not to have children at all. Others, like myself, decided to have children when it suited me with the result that I marked time professionally (by working part-time) from my late 20s until mid 30s. Most professional partnerships see electing to have children as a loss of commitment. They cite client unease and an inability to meet chargeable hours' targets. Partnership agreements are often silent on the position regarding maternity rights. This means that when the situation arises it becomes a very personal and subjective discussion, thus putting the woman on the defensive. I know of a number of extreme results of this, with the individuals affected feeling very disappointed at the attitude of their partners on this issue.

Men with young families also feel under pressure, torn between supporting their business partners and their personal partners, often working long hours and at weekends with the result that they have neither the time nor the energy to be with their family.

8.5.3 What do we need to do to make it?

Not everyone want to become an equity partner with the rewards and worries that role brings. Some professionals prefer to focus on becoming experts in their field, leaving it up to other people to bring in clients and manage money and staff. However, if we do decide that becoming a partner is our ultimate goal, how do we then achieve it?

It is important to make a conscious decision to seek to become a partner. Once that is decided, we need to look for support from our firm to achieve it. As a result, firms need to build a generic career development plan showing the path to partnership. This must highlight the importance of not merely becoming more technically skilled but also the need, from the *outset* of our professional careers, to build our management skills. Yet, in my experience, very few professional firms have a defined career structure arguing that it is impossible to project client service demands five or ten years from now. At the same time, most will agree that finding and keeping good quality professionals is a difficult and ongoing challenge. It is possible to make some projections about what people and skills we will need several years from now. Developing a formal Career Profile is therefore possible and in my view, essential.

We can start by identifying which people we expect to replace, due to their age or life profile. Most partners are in their forties and fifties, so we can expect *at most* twenty more years of their contribution. We can also identify from our Resource Audits and management information where we have too few people and/or expertise. From our Client Service Audits we know what types of service our clients want from us now and potentially in the future. All of this can be built into our People Action Plan. If, for example, we expect 60% of our current partners to retire within the next five years, where will their successors come from? If we are dependent on one key Managing Partner, what will we do if he or she decides to return to purely client work?

A sample of a Career Profile is illustrated in the table at the end of this Chapter. We must look at the steps taken from entry into our firm through to junior, then senior professional, associate/manager and ultimately partner. In most cases, this will span a period of around ten years. It encourages us to look at the focus of our technical and management skills development at each stage as well as how to support that development, for example, through formal coaching and mentoring.

As an entry level professional, we need to concentrate on building our technical competence through learning the practical application of academic theory and gaining an understanding of office practices and procedures. Our management skills will concentrate on developing good time management, prioritisation and teamwork. The best way to support our learning will be through observing more experienced professionals and working alongside them.

As we progress to becoming a junior professional, we will work hard at developing our technical competence by being exposed more directly to clients. We will continue to practice our technical skills with increasing degrees of difficult work. We will concentrate on developing our client skills, such as listening and building their trust. We will be helped through this stage through in-house training, formal CPD requirements and working with more senior professionals.

Once we become more senior, we will be expected to take a more active role in managing people, with an increased emphasis in delegating to and supervising younger professionals. We will have identified areas we want to specialise in and the type of clients and client work we want to develop. We will be expected to not merely apply but also interpret procedures, as well as develop innovative solutions to resolving client problems. We may well be guided by a more experienced colleague who has formally or informally become our mentor. We may opt for a short period of secondment to widen our business skills.

As an Associate or Manager, we will be involved directly in operational decisions and at the same time be expected to build our own client base and expertise. At this stage, we need to concentrate on deepening our understanding of business and commercial issues, which we may achieve through heading up key business projects or operational departments, and/or obtaining external management qualifications.

When we arrive at Partner level, we will be fully involved in the business, understanding strategic issues and overseeing operational management. We will be continuing to build our own external market and client reputation through networking and being *seen* as an expert. We may have decided that we want to use an external coach to allow us to tackle our personal development.

This summary illustrates the incremental steps we have all taken and need to take to develop from a novice professional into a fully-fledged partner. As a result, it helps us plan our career, rather than simply focussing on direct client work. The ability to develop and sustain long-term relationships with clients is one of the essential skills of making partner. However, it is only one. Others must include the ability to work well with colleagues and support staff, and of ensuring work is done profitably and safely.

Conclusions

It is essential to match our shape and structure to our business direction. To achieve this, we need to reward people who behave well, share clients and knowledge. Our shape must increase the energy and innovation of all our people, allowing them to work well together, adding value to our client services.

Mobility in the marketplace is a current threat to our future success as it puts us under pressure to consistently deliver a high quality service. However, mobility also offers us the potential to grow our skill base and adapt our shape to meet future client demands. Succession planning is an essential part of any skill development and must be built into our career progression through to partnership.

Key Action Points

1. make sure that our structure and shape reflects our core values
2. reward people who support our long-term growth
3. ensure that our work environment is energetic and innovative
4. allow people to work well together and encourage them to share
5. do all we can to attract and retain key people and skills
6. build in flexibility into our formal structures
7. be open and impartial in our career progression
8. identify the core attributes of a 'good partner'

Table 8.5.3 Career Profile

	Progression	Focus of Technical skills	Focus of Management skills	How support his/her development?
YEAR 10 Partner	Fully involved in the business	Maintaining external market and client reputation	Strategic management Overseeing operations Networking	External coach
YEAR 8 Associate/ Partner	Moving into direct involvement in business decisions	Continuing to build client base and expertise	Business and commercial understanding	Heading up key business projects or departments Formal management qualification
YEAR 5 Senior	Widening work role into management of people	More specialist work and own client work	Delegating and supervising Making decisions and interpreting procedures Developing innovative solutions	Mentor Short-term secondment
YEARS 2 to 4 Junior	Polishing technical competence and working more directly with clients	Continued practical application with developing degrees of difficulty	Concentrating on developing skills in client service delivery, including listening and building trust Operating in-house procedures consistently	Coach CPD In-house training
YEAR 1 Entry	Building technical competence	Learning the practical application of taught knowledge	Time management Prioritisation Team-working Learning in-house procedures	Line manager In-house training Formal graduate programme

9

PUTTING IT INTO PRACTICE

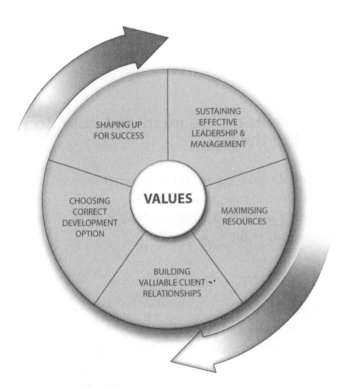

9.1   Introduction

The purpose of this book is fourfold: to save us time, re-assure us, allow us to manage change and finally, implement success. This Chapter focuses on all four by summarising the skills, techniques and tools which allow us to put the Model into practice.

In essence, it summarises the 'how to' use the Model for Success. We have covered the 'why' in depth in Chapters 2 to 8 and looked at external market trends, the need for effective leadership and resource management, the importance of core values, of talking to clients, of selecting and matching the correct development option with our shape and structure. We have considered the need to develop written business and action plans and complete audit checklists. We have looked at the skills required to be effective in a number of roles, including a client-focussed professional and knowledge worker. As a result, the Model has now become three dimensional, fleshed out with information about what we need to do to put it into practice.

This Chapter concentrates on the *application* of the Model to achieve accelerated best practice. It allows us to identify how to use it, apply it and implement it.

9.2   What skills do we need and how do we develop them?

From the outset, we have looked at the importance of implementing change. We have investigated each Segment of the Model, analysing what required to be tackled and why. Each chapter has looked at a number of roles and skills that need to be developed in the context of being:

- a good professional,
- a knowledge professional,
- an innovator,
- an effective leader and manager,
- able to develop long-term client relationships,
- able to understand the market, identify and implement strategic choices,
- able to match our structure with our shape, and
- capable of managing constant change.

As a result, we may now be feeling that we have to be a many-headed Hydra, swivelling each head in turn to face each individual problem we want to deal with. We may also feel that we have to behave differently internally than we do when dealing directly with clients.

First of all, I want to provide reassurance that this is not the case. We do not need to develop a new set of 'management' skills for every problem and situation. The skills we need for managing our client work are exactly the same skills that we need to manage our people. For example, both want us to listen to them and respond with practical solutions to their problems.

Secondly, I want to reinforce the *commonality* of these skills. Regardless of which formal job role we are tackling, there are a number of core skills required. These are split into four distinct areas:

1. the professional and technical skills needed to do our job as professional advisors,
2. those relating to our work organisation,
3. the interpersonal skills we use when working with other people, and
4. our personal skills.

These in turn can be broken down into individual elements which can be used as the basis of career and training development. These are summarised in Table 9.2.

Because they are common to our current roles, they are also *transferable*. This is an important point as many professionals think they can only develop 'management skills' once they hold more senior positions. For example, trainees will argue with me that there is little point in developing their business skills as they are not directly involved in running the business. Similarly, if I ask young professionals how much direct client contact they have, they will tell me *'not a lot, I only write to clients'*. Strangely enough, I am sure the clients will see that as direct contact!

Thirdly, it is much easier to persuade professionals to tackle their skill development in the context of client-service delivery. If we suggest that they have to improve their management skills in isolation, they are often unlikely to see this as an important priority. However, if we suggest that they look at the skills to develop long-term client relationships, which will include of necessity, listening, communicating and managing expectations, they will be much more receptive.

As a result, it is possible to develop these skills throughout our professional career. Using the Career Profile described in Chapter 8 helps people to see the links between each 'job' stage and their incremental skill development. We can learn how to apply these skills, identify those we are naturally good at and those

Table 9.2 Core Skills

1 Professional and technical
• technical excellence
• professional integrity
• commercial awareness
• IT skills
2 Work organisation
• resource maximisation
• source and analyse accurate information
• forward plan, prioritise, work under pressure and deliver to deadlines
• make and implement decisions
• assess and manage risk
3 Interpersonal
• work collaboratively
• share knowledge
• learn and teach
• solve problems in an innovative way
• present solutions persuasively
• manage conflict constructively
• listen, question, respond and give feedback
• communicate well (written and verbal)
4 Personal
• inspire trust
• create empathy
• build long term relationships
• resilience and tenacity
• patience and tolerance
• optimism and adaptability
• self-assurance and self-motivation

where we need some formal or informal help. Formal help can be sourced through training, working through external qualifications, line manager review and coaching. Informal help can include client feedback, peer review or self-reflection.

9.3   What does a successful firm actually do?

Throughout the book, we have talked about professional service firms that have achieved success. They are found in all the professional sectors, and include large regional organisations and small local practices. They all operate in the same way and have developed a core of common practices. I have used these to develop a series of questions detailed in the Table below. Answering these questions will therefore allow us to position our individual firms against the Model for Success.

It is worthwhile scoring ourselves against them for two reasons. First of all it will provide us with reassurance about how far we are along the road to success. Secondly, it will allow us to identify where further work is required.

To do this, we need to consider whether we can answer 'yes' to the questions posed in Table 9.3.

This self-reflective exercise allows us to focus our efforts on areas of priority for our firm. Where we have answered 'yes', it highlights where we are successfully implementing the Model in practice. Where we have said 'no' or are unsure, it helps to identify which of the five Segments requires action and where we need to direct our attention.

As a result, we need to prepare a detailed Action Plan tailored to our own firm. To help us do this and to save readers the time of going back through each Chapter, I have developed a detailed Action Plan that tells us what to do to implement individual Segments (see appendix to this Chapter).

The actions in it are listed in numerical order of implementation. Their application must be tailored to the needs of our individual firms, its size and/or level of sophistication. For example, people managing smaller practices may wish to focus only on the basic Model, the actions for which are printed in bold type. Those managing more complicated or more sophisticated firms will want to consider implementing all of the Actions recommended.

It is also worthwhile considering at this point what frustrates success and causes implementation to stall. This provides us with additional clues about what we must overcome. For example, effective leadership and management will be

Table 9.3 Our position against successful firms

	The Model for Success	Yes/N
	Segment 1	
1	Do we have leaders and managers who are trusted and respected?	
2	Do we have written business plans which we are able to implement?	
3	Do we have a written statement of values which we demonstrate by our behaviour, both internally and externally?	
4	Do we have open and honest communications?	
	Segment 2	
5	Do we have access to accurate, up to date and useful data about operational performance?	
6	Do we use financial performance as a measure of success rather than a driver?	
7	Do we ensure that people work flexibly, share information and help each other?	
8	Do we continually achieve improvements in internal efficiency through effective resource and people management?	
9	Do we continually improve our work practices through integration of technology?	
10	Do we invest and continue to invest in technology and training?	
	Segment 3	
11	Do we carefully select the clients and sectors we work for?	
12	Do we consistently deliver high quality professional services, tailored to the needs of clients and at a level valuable to both parties?	
13	Do we regularly meet clients, check their perception of service delivery, establish what is important to them and their likely future demands?	
14	Do we have a clear client focus and continually change the way we work and the shape of the firm to respond to clients' needs?	

	Segment 4	
15	Do we keep in touch with the marketplace and are able to predict future trends and shifts?	
16	Have we chosen a development option, matched to our values, resources, market and client needs and our brand and reputation?	
17	Have we developed ways of working in partnership with other organisations and are happy to share our expertise and resources?	
	Segment 5	
18	Do we continually adjust our structure and skill base to cope with future changes in demands?	
19	Have we developed and apply clear objective career profiles, including succession planning?	
20	Are we able to implement change?	

frustrated by fear and mistrust. People will not use resources well when they are too tired to think clearly or too much of their energy is taken up with fire fighting. Long-term relationships will not be possible where promises made to clients are not kept. Development options will become irrelevant where people over analyse ideas and take too long to make a decision. Changes to our structure and shape cannot happen without the understanding and involvement of everyone. It is essential therefore to use all of our techniques and tools to make change happen.

For example, our Values exercise will instil openness and trust. Our Plans will allow people to use their time and energy effectively. Audits will enable us to know what we do well and how we can improve on our strengths. Our Action Points focus our decisions and define what we must do. Stories allow everyone to understand what we represent and demonstrate what we actually do. This brings us full circle to the core importance of our values. Values sit in the centre of the Model for Success. We must work with people and clients who share our values. We must select development options and ensure that our shape and structure match them. We must use stories to illustrate our values and what we believe in.

9.4   Techniques and tools

Each Chapter has described a range of techniques and tools designed to implement key sections. These save us time and provide us with something concrete *to do* rather than talk about doing. They also provide us with a structure to tackle key issues in a way that will produce something tangible. This allows us to show that change is possible and that something concrete has been achieved.

Each technique brings with it particular attributes. For example, Audits help us analyse and identify gaps. Exercises provide a mechanism to debate sensitive issues in an informed way.

These techniques therefore include:

1.   **Exercises** to help us resolve tensions and clarify misunderstandings,
2.   **Plans and Written Statements** to allow us to be clear and consistent about what we set out to achieve,
3.   **Audits** to analyse certain operations and identify future actions and priorities,
4.   **Formal Roles** to re-inforce the importance of key activities,
5.   **Training** to raise the profile of key areas and ensure consistency of understanding,
6.   **Action Points** to focus attention on key priorities, and
7.   **Stories** to encapsulate in a memorable and unique way what we have achieved, what we believe in and what we aspire to.

We have also developed a series of tools, particular and relevant to each Segment of the Model. These tools allow us to tackle in a practical way many of the challenges we have discussed.

Table 9.4 groups the techniques and tools cross-referenced to their Chapter sources.

As a result, it is possible to tackle a range of techniques at one and the same time, using them to develop individual Project Plans which include a range of people. For instance, it is perfectly possible to appoint:

1.   Key Client Partners to carry out the Client Service Audit, and develop

Table 9.4 Techniques and Tools cross referenced to each Chapter

Techniques	Tools
Exercises	Values Exercise Ch 2
	Commercial versus professional Matrix Ch 2
	Option Debate Exercise Ch 2
	Practicality Check of our values and resources Ch 2
	Structure Mapping Exercise Ch 2
	Formal People Appraisals Ch 2 and Ch 8
	Knowledge Management capture Ch and Ch 8
	Relationship Map Ch 4
	Conflict Map showing hot and cold, people and process Ch 4
	Risk Workload Matrix Ch 5
	How clients define exceptional service Ch 6
	Values of potential merger partners Ch 7
Plans and written statements	Commonality of Purpose Ch 2
	Business Plan Ch 2
	Career Profile including succession Ch 2 and Ch 8
	Partner Profile Ch 2 and Ch 8
	Job Profiles Ch 2
	Behaviour Policy Statement Ch 4
	Risk Management Policy Ch 5
	Definition of high quality service Ch 5
	Statement of Staff Support Ch 5
	Good Behaviour Statement Ch 8
Audits	SWOT Analysis Ch 2
	Resource Audit and Action Plan Ch 2
	Client Service Audit and Action Plan Ch 2
	Market Analysis Ch 2 and Ch 7
	Skills Audit and People Action Plan Ch 2, Ch 5 and Ch 8
	Time Audit Ch 5
	Meeting Audit Ch 5
	Risk Assessment Analysis Ch 5
Formal Roles	Key Client Partners Ch 2
	Strategy Group (or individual) Ch 2 and Ch 7
	External consultant Ch 3
	Internal Risk Checker Ch 5

Table 9.4 Techniques and Tools cross referenced to each Chapter (cont.)

Techniques	Tools
Training	Secondment Ch 2 and Ch 8 Selling training Ch 6 Formal pitch presentations Ch 6 Talking about money training Ch 6 Formal management qualifications Ch 8
Action Points	Key Action Points all Chapters Self-diagnostic Action Plan Ch 9
Stories	About values Ch 4 About our success Ch 4 Examples of what we can achieve for clients Ch 6

     success Stories,

2.   the Strategy Group to manage the Market Analysis, generate some development ideas and tackle some development options,

3.   the Internal Risk Checker to develop the Risk Management Policy, Risk Assessment Analysis and Risk Workload Matrix, working in association with individual fee earners or Heads of Department,

4.   the Staff or Training Partner to complete the Skills Audit, develop the written Behaviour Policy Statement, the Statement of Staff Support, the Partner and Career Profiles, and organise the internal training courses, leaving

5.   the management team to concentrate on strategic issues, such as agreeing the core Values, Commonality of Purpose and the Business Plan with the key stakeholders, and operational matters, such as the SWOT analysis, Resource, Time and Meetings Audits, and the Operational Structure, Influencers and Conflict Maps.

As always, it is important to target and tackle key priorities as we have only limited time, energy and resources. It is also important to remain flexible.

9.5   Flexible and adaptable

One final area requires practical discussion. The Model for Success is designed to allow us to manage and implement change. To do this, we must be able to manage a continuous series of contradictions as the market, clients, regulations, technology, resources, and people do not remain constant. For example, key people in our firm may leave, new regulations may require internal management systems, and major clients may merge and as a result, choose new advisers. As a result, we will often feel that just as we have resolved one problem, another one appears in its place. We must be able to be flexible and adaptable enough to conduct a balancing act between one pressure and another.

From our earlier analysis, we know that to remain competitive today we must do more than provide quality professional services. Our clients, as the end users of our service, have become much more critical of their professionals. In addition, profit margins are under pressure for most professional firms. As a result, we need to be able to provide exceptional professional service cost effectively with few instances of mistakes. Increasingly, as technology impacts on the way that we work, we have to use our expertise and experience to interpret rather than process information. We need to 'add value' to our clients so that they in return value us for the support we provide. As a result, our people provide our competitive edge – the way they tackle clients' demands and the approach they take. All areas of our firms need to work well together to provide the *'seamless and consistent'* approach that is part of exceptional service. To achieve this, people need to be open with each other, share information, acknowledge when mistakes are made and over and above all, be prepared to change and adapt. The Model for Success allows us to tackle continuous change in an informed and structured way and as a result, achieve accelerated best practice.

Conclusions

This Chapter summarises the Model for Success in action. The skills required to implement it successfully are common to both our internal and external roles. Working through each Segment encourages us to identify key priorities, as well as the techniques and tools to put the theory into practice.

Accelerated best practice is possible and results from becoming comfortable with change, and successfully implementing a range of development techniques. Effective leadership and management are crucial as professionals will only allow themselves to be managed by people they trust. Values are the core to each Segment as they drive our decision-making, communications and professionalism. Using our resources well requires us to work effectively, sharing our skills, knowledge and clients. We must focus on building long-term relationships with our clients, where both sides see benefits and value. We must concentrate our energy and innovation on choosing the right development option for our firm, our values and resources. Our shape and structure must match what we believe in and what we want to achieve.

Key Action Points

1.   remind people that our core skills are common and transferable
2.   tackle skill development in a structured and incremental way
3.   benchmark ourselves against 'successful firms'
4.   develop a detailed Action Plan to implement the Model
5.   do not allow change to stall
6.   focus on doing rather than talking
7.   develop Project Plans for named individual(s)
8.   implement accelerated best practice

Appendix – Detailed Action Plan

The actions below are listed in numerical order of implementation. Their application must be tailored to the needs of each individual firm, its size and/or its level of sophistication. For example, people managing smaller practices may wish to focus only on the basic Model, the actions for which are **printed in bold type.** Those managing more complicated or more sophisticated firms will want to consider implementing all of the Actions recommended.

Segment 1 Sustaining effective leadership and management
1. **appoint leaders and managers who are trusted and respected, have core skills of financial, people and strategic management, and understand the marketplace and client development**
2. **if recruiting managers from outside our own professional network, emphasise their CVs and previous track-record to establish their credibility.**
3. **concentrate on listening to people and building long-term relationships**
4. identify the key influencers within our organisations, involve them in our projects and discussions, build bridges with them to improve communications and reduce conflict
5. **complete a Values Exercise to agree our core values, address any underlying tensions this exercise throws up, such as a perceived conflict between being professional and being commercial**
6. **develop a written Commonality of Purpose Statement**
7. **develop a written Business Plan, updated regularly with which everyone is familiar and which is used as the basis of all decision taking**
8. **demonstrate our adherence to our core values in a tangible way through reward mechanisms, job descriptions, individual achievements, websites, recruitment, specific projects and the stories we tell**
9. develop a written Behaviour Policy Statement which defines good behaviour and include its elements in job descriptions, reviews etc, reward and communicate the facts about peoples' contribution to the firm
10. **tackle bad behaviour by dealing with conflict constructively, establish the facts, map out areas of tension, identify whether process or people issues and find solutions to problems**
11. **ensure that we communicate information in a way that people find useful, and develop stories which reflect our values and what we**

believe in
12. encourage professionalism through projects which focus on:
- knowledge management, sharing, learning
- finding innovative solutions to client feedback, market trend analysis, resource bottlenecks, system development
- developing a learning culture, tackling mistakes and risk management,
- building integrity, tolerance, patience, empathy, optimism and adaptability

13. **be comfortable with managing dichotomy, including being:-**
- **flexible, able to identify opposing pressures and balance them**
- **able to recruit the best and manage them**
- **cost effective and tailored in our service delivery**
- **client responsive yet retaining control over workloads**
- **careful and innovative , and**
- **willing to use outsiders to help and support *us***

Segment 2 Maximising our resources
1. **involve as many people as possible in completing a Resource Audit to provide data about our resources which is accurate, up to date and impartial**
2. **complete a SWOT analysis, focus on our strengths and implement actions to tackle our weaknesses**
3. **ensure that we operate effective financial management, including cash flow, recoverability, work in progress values, profitability**
4. **prioritise projects which *release* resources, for example, time, systems, styles, IT training and which we can implement quickly**
5. **ensure that performance remuneration encourages reciprocity, sharing and good behaviour**
6. **always check resources against action plans and projects to ensure that we have sufficient time, people, skills, energy to implement them**
7. **complete a Time Audit to focus on people's use of time, for example, why targets are not being met, if people working too long hours, identify bottlenecks and time stealers, emails and meetings**
8. develop a policy which requires internal emails to be batched and sent at the beginning and/or end of the working day
9. complete a Meeting Audit and reduce the number of internal meetings, revisit who attends, timings, agendas and process,

10. focus on client outcomes (rather than service processes), delivered with speed, accuracy and consistency
11. develop a Risk Management Policy which addresses stress and allows people make mistakes and learn from them
12. introduce client management through client selection and develop a formal Risk Assessment analysis based on client and/or work type
13. develop a Risk Workload Analysis to weigh risk against reward, as well as identify work which can be used for training, delegation and professional development
14. appoint an internal 'Risk Checker' who looks for 'what if' situations
15. write down and publish our definition of what constitutes high quality service and what help is available for staff career development

Segment 3 Building valuable client relationships
1. regularly complete a Client Service Audit, respond to clients' comments by adjusting our services, systems and training to improve at a minimum, the speed and consistency of our service delivery
2. ask clients what future services they will require and how they will want them delivered and build these into our future development
3. manage clients' expectations up front, send out clear letters of engagement, ensure our people talk about costs, timescales etc with them, develop in-house training and handouts/flowcharts of procedures to give to clients
4. ask key clients what they define as exceptional, agree service levels tailored to them, focus on solving problems and finding innovative, valuable solutions
5. concentrate on developing our listening skills
6. implement effective cross selling by:-
    • providing people with basic information about each other and what other departments achieve for clients
    • run in-house cross service function presentations and educate people about what we mean by 'selling'
    • develop literature which focuses on the benefits our services bring to clients and what distinguishes us from our competitors
    • preserve a three-way relationship between original referrer, client and new professional or department
    • ensure our reward mechanism values cross selling
7. ensure that all formal pitches for work are fully prepared for, focus on

the context of what we do and provide real life examples of what we can achieve for clients

8.   use informal networking in a way that people feel comfortable with
9.   develop success stories to demonstrate what we say we do
10.   make sure that all of our marketing and branding reinforces our personality

Segment 4 Choosing the correct development option
1.   be aware of the marketplace and be able to identify future trends and shifts
2.   set up a Strategy Group to complete regular market analysis, report findings, identify current trends which require short, medium and long-term responses and how we intend to manage them
3.   encourage both left and right-brained thinking
4.   use an external strategic model to sort trends and identify priorities
5.   build in what our clients will want from their professional service providers in the future, what matches our values and resources into our final option selection
6.   select one development option, check that we have the management skills to do it, support its strengths and address its weaknesses and focus our Strategy Group on supporting it
7.   if seeking accelerated growth, increase our resource base, management and networking skills
8.   if seeking a merger partner, first of all check that our values are compatible
9.   consider expansion as a development option, focusing on what we are good at and enjoy doing, and keeping a look out for opportunities and synergies
10.   develop an Action Plan to achieve implementation which is realistic in terms of timescales, resources and personnel
11.   make sure that our market positioning, image, brand and reputation all support our choice

Segment 5 Shaping up for success
1.   map out and adjust our operational structure to ensure that it is clear, understood and followed by everyone
2.   complete a Skills Audit to identify under and oversupply of key skills, and to provide a focus for our recruitment and people development,

develop a People Action Plan to close any gaps and provide future resource base

3. introduce regular workload and individual development reviews, train line managers, appoint coaches and mentors, pay attention to 'distress flares', talk to people regularly to find out underlying problems

4. instil energy and innovation, ensure that we build in flexibility and the ability to change and reward people for doing so

5. manage the current mobility in the marketplace by:-
    - first checking whether we can prevent it
    - if not, manage people who are leaving in a positive way, and
    - identify what opportunities have been created for restructuring and/or new skills

6. develop written Partner and Job Profiles, introduce skills training, develop Career Profile, succession plans and secondment opportunities

7. **develop a clearly defined selection process, ensure there are no 'favourites' or 'fiefdoms' and reward long term commitment**

8. encourage people to tackle a variety of work and gain external qualifications

9. adjust our structure and shape to support our future direction

REFERENCES

Debra M Amidon, *The Ken Awakening – innovation strategy for the Knowledge Economy* (Boston: Butterworth-Heinemann, 1997)

Ron Ashkenas, Dave Ulrich, Todd Jick, & Steve Kerr, *The Boundaryless Organization – breaking the chains of organizational structure* (San Francisco: Jossey-Bass, 1995)

David Armstrong, *Managing by Storying Around: the new method of leadership* (New York: Doubleday, 1992)

Alan Barker, *The Alchemy of Innovation – perspectives from the leading edge* (London: Spiro Press, 2002)

Peter Bolt, *Coaching for Growth – how to bring out the best in your team and yourself* (Dublin: Oak Tree Press, 2000)

Tony Buzan, *The Mind Map Book* (London: BCA, 1993)

Margaret Cauley de la Sierra, *Managing Global Alliances – key steps for successful collaboration* (Wokingham: Addison-Wesley Publishing Company, 1995)

Subir Chowdhury (ed.) *Management 21C* (London: Pearson Education Limited, 2000)

Don Cohen, & Laurence Prusak, *In Good Company – how social capital makes organizations work* (Boston: Harvard Business School Press, 2001)

Robert Cooper, & Ayman Sawaf, *Executive EQ – emotional intelligence in business* (London: Orion Business Books, 1997)

Mick Cope, *Leading the organisation to learn – the 10 levers for putting knowledge and learning to work* (London: Financial Times Management, 1998)

James W Cortada, *Rise of the Knowledge Worker* (Boston: Butterworth-Heinemann 1998)

Thomas H Davenport, & Laurence Prusak, *Working Knowledge – how organizations manage what they know* (Boston: Harvard Business School Press, 2000)

Arie De Geus, *The Living Company – growth, learning and longevity in business* (London: Nicholas Brealey Publishing Limited, 1999)

Yves L Doz & Gary Hamel, *Alliance Advantage – the art of creating value through partnering* (Boston: Harvard Business School Press, 1998)

Leif Edvinsson, *Corporate Longitude – what you need to know to navigate the knowledge economy* (London: Pearson Education Limited, 2002)

Leif Edvinsson & Michael S Malone, *Intellectual Capital – the proven way to establish your company's real value by measuring its hidden brainpower* (London: Judy Piatkus (Publishers) Limited, 1997)

Lynne Eisaguirre, *The Power of a Good Fight – how to embrace conflict to drive productivity, creativity and innovation* (Indianapolis: Alpha Books, 2002)

Daniel Goleman, *Working with Emotional Intelligence* (London: Bloomsbury, 1998)

Michael Hammer, *Beyond Re-engineering – how the process-centred organisation is changing our work and our lives* (London: Harper Collins Business, 1988)

Manfred Kets de Vries, *The Leadership Mystique – a user's manual to human enterprise* (London: Pearson Education Limited, 2001)

Georg von Krogh, Johan Roos & Dirk Kleine (eds.) *Knowing Firms – understanding, managing and measuring knowledge* (London: Sage, 1998)

Dorothy Leonard & Walter Swap, *When Sparks Fly – igniting creativity in groups* (Boston: Harvard Business School Press, 1999)

David Maister, *True Professionalism* (New York: The Free Press, 1997) and *The Trusted Adviser* (New York: The Free Press, 2000)

Mitchell Lee Marks & Philip H Mirvis, *Joining Forces – making one plus one equal three in mergers, acquisitions and alliances* (San Francisco: Jossey-Bass Publishers, 1998)

Henry Mintzberg, *The Rise and Fall of Strategic Planning* (Harvard Business Review, Jan – Feb (1994) p107)

David Molden, *NLP Business Masterclass – skills for realizing human potential* (London: Pearson Education Limited, 2001)

Nigel Nicholson, *Managing the Human Animal* (London: Texere Publishing Limited, 2000)

Monica Nicou, Christine Ribbing & Eva Ading *Sell Your Knowledge – The Professional's Guide to Winning More Business* (London: Kogan Page Limited, 1994)

Roger Osborne, *The Floating Egg – Episodes in the Making of Geology* (London: Pimlico, 1999)

Paul E Plsek, *Creativity, Innovation and Quality* ASQC (Milwaukee, Wisconsin: Quality Press, 1997)

Michael E Porter *Competitive Strategy: Techniques for Analysing Industries and Competition* (New York: Free Press, 1980)

Craig Pritchard, Richard Hull, Mike Chumer & Hugh Willmott (eds.) *Managing Knowledge – critical investigations of work and learning* (London: Macmillan Business, 2000)

Stephen Reid, *How to think – building your mental muscle* (London: Prentice Hall, 2002)

Michael Schrage, *No More Teams – mastering the dynamics of creative collaboration* (New York: Currency Doubleday, 1989)

Larraine Segil, Marshall Goldsmith, & James Belasco (eds) *Partnering – the new face of leadership* (New York: AMACOM, 2003)

S Tilles *Making Strategy Explicit* in I Ansoff, *Business Strategy* (London: Penguin, 1968)

Fiona Westwood *Achieving Best Practice – shaping professionals for success* (Maidenhead: McGraw-Hill, 2001)

(Those printed in bold are particularly worthwhile reading)

INDEX

Lightning Source UK Ltd.
Milton Keynes UK
UKOW06f1106131215

264626UK00001B/16/P

9 781785 891076